TECHNIQUES IN MARRIAGE AND FAMILY COUNSELING

■ Volume Two ■

Edited by
Richard E. Watts

THE FAMILY PSYCHOLOGY AND COUNSELING SERIES

■■■

Developed Collaboratively by the American Counseling Association and
the International Association of Marriage and Family Counselors

TECHNIQUES IN MARRIAGE AND FAMILY COUNSELING, VOLUME TWO

10 9 8 7 6 5 4 3 2 1

American Counseling Association
5999 Stevenson Avenue
Alexandria, VA 22304

Director of Publications
Carolyn C. Baker

Production Manager
Bonny E. Gaston

Copy Editor
Ida Audeh

Cover design by Martha Woolsey

Library of Congress Cataloging-in-Publication Data

Techniques in marriage and family counseling, Volume Two / edited
    by Richard E. Watts
        p. cm. (The family psychology and counseling series)
    Includes bibliographical references.
    ISBN 1-55620-212-1 (alk. paper)
    1. Marriage counseling. 2. Family counseling I. Watts, Richard E.
II. Series.

HQ10. T39 2001
362. 82' 86—dc21   99-32975
                                                                      CIP

The Family Psychology and Counseling Series

Understanding Stepfamilies: Implications for Assessment and Treatment
Debra Huntley, PhD

In Preparation

African American Family Counseling
Jo-Ann Lipford Sanders, PhD, and Carla Bradley, PhD

Practical Approaches for School Counselors: Integrating Family Counseling in School Settings
Lynn D. Miller, PhD

Advisory Board

■ ■ ■

THE FAMILY PSYCHOLOGY AND COUNSELING SERIES

Table of Contents

From the Series Editor

Volume Two of *Techniques in Marriage and Family Counseling* provides additional practical strategies. The volume is divided into three sections: cognitive and constructivist–constructionist framework; structural and strategic orientation; and working with parent–child relationships. Each section offers ideas that can be easily modified for use by practitioners of all theoretical persuasions.

I enjoy the opportunity to learn from the creativity of these contributors. Although I do not use their ideas verbatim, they are easy to tailor to my own method of therapy. I hope you are also able to grow your own therapy interventions from these suggestions. I also hope that you have read *Techniques in Marriage and Family Counseling*, Volume One.

Congratulations to Richard Watts and his contributors for another job well done.

—*Jon Carlson, PsyD, EdD*
Series Editor

Preface

Volume Two of *Techniques in Marriage and Family Counseling* is a collection of techniques adapted and modified by experienced couple and family counselors. As with Volume One, the techniques contained herein stem from various theoretical perspectives but focus on practical utility. Part I addresses techniques from cognitive and constructivist or constructionist frameworks. Part II presents techniques stemming from structural and strategic orientations. Part III contains couple and family play therapy techniques and techniques that address various aspects of parent–child relationships.

As noted in the preface to Volume One, the techniques included in the present volume are "general working versions" (Sherman & Fredman, 1985, p. xii). In other words, the technique discussion does not include specific applications that each counselor must make in order to best serve the unique couples and families that he or she serves. Couple and family counselors are an immensely creative group. The contributors to this and the previous volume introduce some clever twists and interesting adaptations to foundational ideas in couple and family counseling. I hope that these techniques are useful for practitioners in helping clients to tap into their own creativity in regard to technique development and refinement.

—*Richard E. Watts, PhD*

Reference

Sherman, R., & Fredman, N. (1985). *Handbook of structured techniques in marriage and family therapy.* New York: Brunner/Mazel.

■ ■ ■

Biographies

Richard E. Watts, PhD, is an associate professor of counseling in the Department of Educational Psychology at Baylor University in Waco, Texas. He received his PhD in counseling from the University of North Texas. Prior to joining the Baylor faculty in 2000, Dr. Watts held faculty positions at Texas A&M University—Commerce and Kent State University. Dr. Watts has authored more than 50 professional articles and book chapters and 2 books, and he currently serves on the editorial board of several professional journals. His current interests include Adlerian, cognitive, and constructive approaches to individual and couple and family counseling, counselor supervision and counselor efficacy, ethical and legal issues, play therapy, and religious and spirituality issues. Dr. Watts and his wife, Cheryl, have one child.

Jon Carlson, PsyD, EdD, is distinguished professor at Governors State University in University Park, Illinois, and director of the Lake Geneva Wellness Clinic in Wisconsin. He is the founding editor of *The Family Journal: Counseling and Therapy for Couples and Families* and has served as president of the International Association of Marriage and Family Counselors. Dr. Carlson holds a diplomat in family psychology from the American Board of Professional Psychology. He is a fellow of the American Psychological Association and a certified sex therapist by the American Association of Sex Educators, Counselors, and Therapists. He has written more than 25 books and 125 professional articles. He has received numerous awards for his professional contributions from major professional organizations, including the American Counseling Association, the Association for Counselor Education and Supervision, and the American Psychological Association. Dr. Carson and his spouse of 32 years, Laura, are the parents of five children and grandparents of two.

Contributors

Michael L. Baltimore, PhD, is an associate professor in the Department of Counseling and Educational Leadership at Columbus State University, Columbus, Georgia.

James Robert Bitter, EdD, is a professor in the Department of Human Development and Learning, East Tennessee State University, Johnson City, Tennessee.

Brian S. Canfield, EdD, is a professor and department head in the Department of Human Development, Southeastern Louisiana State University, Hammond, Louisiana.

Michael J. Carter, PhD, is an associate professor and director of the Counseling and Assessment Clinic in the Charter School of Education, California State University, Los Angeles, California.

Frank M. Dattilio, PhD, is a clinical associate in psychiatry at the Center for Cognitive Therapy, University of Pennsylvania School of Medicine. He is also a clinical psychologist in private practice and the clinical director of the Center for Integrative Psychotherapy in Allentown, Pennsylvania.

Phyllis Erdman, PhD, is a professor and department head in the Department of Counseling, Texas A&M University, Commerce, Texas.

William P. Evans, PhD, is an associate professor in the Department of Human Development and Family Studies, University of Nevada, Reno, Nevada.

Marsha Wiggins Frame, PhD, is an associate professor in the Counseling Psychology and Counselor Education Division, University of Colorado at Denver, Denver, Colorado.

Michael Furois, PsyD, is a counseling psychologist at Fort Meade V.A. Medical Center and is an adjunct professor of counseling at South Dakota State University in Brookings, South Dakota.

Karin B. Jordan, PhD, is an assistant professor in the Department of Counseling, Greenspun College of Urban Affairs, University of Nevada, Las Vegas, Nevada.

Frances Y. Mullis, PhD, is an associate professor in the Department of Counseling and Psychological Services, Georgia State University, Atlanta, Georgia.

Michael S. Nystul, PhD, is a professor in the Department of Counseling and Educational Psychology, New Mexico State University, Las Cruces, New Mexico.

Patricia Parr, PhD, is an associate professor in the Department of Counseling and Special Education, University of Akron, Akron, Ohio.

Richard J. Riordan, PhD, is a professor in the Department of Counseling and Psychological Services, Georgia State University, Atlanta, Georgia.

Robert Sherman, EdD, is professor emeritus, Queens College, New York, and resides in Monroe Township, New Jersey.

Robert L. Smith, PhD, is professor and counseling program doctoral chair in the Department of Professional Studies, Texas A&M University, Corpus Christi, Texas.

Johanna E. Soet, MA, is a senior faculty associate in the Rollins School of Public Health, Emory University, Atlanta, Georgia.

Patricia Stevens, PhD, is an associate professor and director of marriage and family training in the Counseling Psychology and

Counselor Education Division, University of Colorado at Denver, Denver, Colorado.

Daniel S. Sweeney, PhD, is an assistant professor in the Counseling Program, George Fox University, Portland, Oregon.

William M. Walsh, PhD, is a professor in the Division of Professional Psychology, University of Northern Colorado, Greeley, Colorado.

S. Allen Wilcoxon, EdD, is a professor and chair of the Counselor Education Program, University of Alabama, Tuscaloosa, Alabama.

Carmen Braun Williams, PhD, is an assistant professor in the Counseling Psychology and Counselor Education Division, University of Colorado at Denver, Denver, Colorado.

John Zarski, PhD, is a professor and department chair in the Department of Counseling and Special Education, University of Akron, Akron, Ohio.

I

COGNITIVE AND CONSTRUCTIVE TECHNIQUES

The first chapter ("Letter for a Change: Using Letter Writing in Marriage and Family Counseling"), by James Robert Bitter, discusses the use of letter writing in couple and family counseling—specifically, letters of conflict disengagement and celebration and letters to mark therapeutic progress. The first two examples he provides are letters written and exchanged between partners or family members, whereas the third is a letter that a counselor writes to clients. The author explains the purpose, process, and utility of these letters in working with couples and families. Although the intervention must be used judiciously, letter writing can serve as a powerful bridge between partners, family members, and counselors and clients.

In chapter 2 ("Therapeutic Correspondence: Writing to Make a Point With Notes and Letters"), Richard J. Riordan and Johanna E. Soet focus on the counselor's use of therapeutic correspondence in working with couples and families. The authors begin by identifying theoretical support for and discussing the unique aspects of letter writing in counseling. Then they identify and provide examples of various forms of therapeutic correspondence, discuss logistical issues involved, and conclude by presenting the advantages and disadvantages of using letter writing as an intervention. As the authors note, this pantheoretical approach integrates easily into any counselor's approach to couples and family counseling.

In chapter 3 ("Split Team Therapy"), Brian S. Canfield presents split team therapy (STT), a constructive adaptation of a supervision team technique pioneered by members of the Milan Family Institute. Canfield describes the approach as a collaborative process between clients, the counselor, and the supervision team that avoids many of the potential problems of direct counselor–client agreement or disagreement on any issue in counseling. The therapeutic process of STT facilitates the formation and shifting of therapeutic alliances so that multiple perspectives on presenting issues are considered.

Using actual reflecting teams in couple and family counseling is sometimes not logistically or financially possible. In chapter 4 ("Using Imaginary Team Members in Couples Counseling"), Richard E. Watts addresses an alternative constructive "team" approach; that is, using imaginary team members in couples counseling. Using imaginary teams can help clients step out of or away from presenting problems. By consulting team members, clients may create a place for reflection in order to develop perceptual alternatives, exceptions, and unique or preferred outcomes.

Chapter 5 ("Conveying the 'Not Knowing' Position in Marriage and Family Counseling"), by Phyllis Erdman, discusses how counselors can convey the "not knowing" position in family counseling. This approach, which posits that clients are the "experts" of their lives, shifts the role of counselors from expert to collaborator. Thus, the "not knowing" or "one down position" focuses on clients' feedback, conveys confidence in clients' strengths and abilities, and helps clients co-create possibilities for change.

In the sixth chapter ("Womanist Interventions: Working With African American Women in Couples and Family Therapy"), Marsha Wiggins Frame and Carmen Braun Williams discuss counseling themes based on the unique experiences of African American women. According to the authors, numerous interventions from the "womanist" perspective address the interrelationship among the experiences of African American women in terms of race, gender, community, family, and spirituality. Frame and Williams present interventions addressing issues of spirituality and race as they affect African American women and their families.

Counselors working with couples often struggle with the problem of one partner interrupting the other in self-defense or to make a point. In chapter 7 ("Pad and Pencil Technique"), Frank M. Dattilio presents a technique that helps impulsive partners wait their turn.

The pad and pencil technique encourages in-session note taking by listening partners to help decrease interruptions and keep track of information they deem important.

Michael L. Baltimore, in chapter 8 ("Brief Cognitive Couple Therapy: Thoughtful Solutions"), presents solution-focused brief therapy (SFBT) as a natural accompaniment to cognitive therapy in working with couples. Both approaches emphasize changing the "viewing" (perceptions and cognitions) and the "doing" (behavioral change), but SFBT places great emphasis on looking for strengths and abilities the couple already have. Baltimore explains how the two approaches may be integrated and presents a framework for using them in brief cognitive couple therapy.

Genograms are a commonly used information-gathering tool in couple and family counseling. In chapter 9 ("Modernizing the Genogram: Solutions and Constructions"), Patricia Stevens discusses using genograms from a social constructionist perspective. She describes how counselors can use the genogram to help clients look for and create exceptions and unique outcomes, and she discusses using the genogram as a visual means of documenting therapeutic progress.

In the final chapter of Part I ("Using Solution-Focused Techniques With Reconstructed Family Systems"), Robert L. Smith addresses the use of selected techniques in working with blended or "reconstructed" family systems. Reconstructed families have unique issues, and counselors must be aware of these issues in choosing their interventions. Working from a solution-focused brief therapy perspective, Smith describes how counselors can help family members identify strengths and assets, discover exceptions, and track family progress.

1

Letter for a Change: Using Letter Writing in Marriage and Family Counseling

James Robert Bitter, EdD

Counseling and psychotherapy, whether with individuals, groups, couples, or families, is founded on human interaction and facilitated most often by the nurturance of caring human contact. It is well documented in the helping professions' literature that proximity, intimacy, and genuineness must characterize the therapeutic relationship to facilitate any useful change in clients' lives (Becvar & Becvar, 1996; Bitter & Corey, 2001; Gazda et al., 1999; Greenberg & Johnson, 1988; Horne & Passmore, 1996; Nichols & Schwartz, 1998). To be sure, proximity and human contact are often valuable in the creation of genuine intimacy and possibilities for change. Anything that can be useful, however, has the potential for misuse; for example, human closeness is present in both love and war. Distance is as natural a part of human relationships as closeness, and in most cases a balance of the two is essential. Some advantages of distance include time to (a) disengage from negative interactions, (b) reflect and work through internal conflicts, (c) organize and present one's thoughts and feelings, (d) consider what is needed and what is best for self and others, and (e) develop alternatives and options to current functioning. Putting something off is different than "blowing" something off. Real change almost never occurs in the heat of "battle"; it is more often than not the result of "cooler" reflection.

The written letter has long been used to achieve closeness and contact at a distance. When great writers, thinkers, personalities, or lovers achieve a certain amount of fame, the public often wants to know more about them. It is not uncommon that a sense of intimacy is gained with these people by reading their published letters. When couples are separated or family members are away (e.g., at camp, on vacation, or at war), letters serve as a bridge across physical or emotional distances.

Young love is often ignited in letters "that speak the heart's truth" when the person would be otherwise voiceless or awkward. Even the most private men are often able to express their soul in letters or poetry. However, these types of expressions often become the artifacts of a new and blossoming relationship.

When a family member turns to "letters" to stimulate or renew romance, resolve conflicts, bridge a current distance, or celebrate a special occasion, the current use can be enhanced when the receiver has a memory of earlier "love notes." Whether such letters are suggested by counselors and therapists or emanate from within the writer, the letters give both the sender and the receiver a potential bridge to a better place. Below are some examples and additional discussion of "letters for a change."

Letters for a Change of Heart

Dear Helen,

I don't know if this happens to others, but I always seem to think better after we stop fighting than I do while in the middle of everything. I'm off by myself now, and I have a pretty good idea of what I really wanted to say, what I should have said from the beginning.

You believe that I had no right to tell your mother that "deep down you wanted to spend the holidays with her," to try and patch things up. You are angry at me for interfering and still hurt from the last visit we had at your mom's house. You wish that I wouldn't always try to fix everything that goes wrong and that I would just listen when you bring up problems, not rush to fix them. You're really upset with your mom, and you want me to understand that and stay out of it. I embarrassed you when I called her and made it very difficult for you to handle this problem in the manner you want to. And mostly, you want me to know that my good intentions don't count. I "spilt the milk," and now you have to clean it up.

There is no question that all too often I try to fix things, rather than just listen to you, understand, and let you handle it. You are right about that. I want to talk some more about this later, but mostly I want you to know that I have heard you, and I understand.

Tom

How did Tom come to write such a letter? It is really a letter of disengagement. He is calling the fight off, and he is doing so after some reflection. So why couldn't he have done or said the same thing from the beginning?

Couples and families often develop routines (or patterns) whereby they handle everyday life. Routines and patterns practiced over time tend to become fixed, complete with rules that are essentially impossible to ignore. When couples and families engage in useful routines, they experience a sense of familiarity, comfort, and security. Unfortunately, useless ways of interacting also are prone to develop into patterned responses in the life of a couple or family. Most couple-fights follow a pattern so familiar that, on calmer reflection, the participants can sense when a fight is coming and know how it will start, who will say what to whom, and even how it will eventually end. Couples too often act as if they feel obligated to carry a fight through to an all-too-familiar end, like a bad habit that one finds hard to break.

The topics of couple-fights may change, but the underlying themes are often the same: the belief that each individual knows what is "good/bad/right/wrong." When the process kicks in, it often blocks two essential ingredients for effective resolution: listening and clear thinking. After the fight is over, one or both of the participants generally know what they really wanted to say; in a calmer state, it is even possible to see the other person's point of view. "Talking over" the process of the fight may bring it to resolution. However, it is equally likely to rekindle the motivations and feelings that launched the fight in the first place.

In the aftermath of a fight, a letter to one's partner or mate has many advantages over talking further: (a) the writer can organize and present complete thoughts that are not distracted by interruption; (b) writing in a calmer state may allow for the reflection necessary to write in a manner the partner reader is able to receive; (c) a letter written, unlike words spoken, does not have to be sent immediately: It can be refined, re-written, or even scrapped altogether; (d) a letter gives the reader time to reflect, lowering the probability of an instant and often patterned reaction; and (e) a caring letter invites a carefully considered response and changes the original pattern of most fights. Most important, a letter is a great way to express a change of heart.

When Tom had time to think about what he wanted to say, he realized that a very important part of what Helen was saying was true, and he admitted it. He presented his admission in specific detail, so that Helen could really know she was heard. Most important, he did not placate Helen with guilt feelings or solemn promises of acting better in the future. He simply recognized the validity of what she was saying and acknowledged it.

Most successful letters with the goal of transforming a fight include the following:

- letting the other person know that they have been heard;
- acknowledging parts of the other person's position that are right, useful, or on target;
- admitting the parts of your position that are wrong or not so useful;
- opening the door to change, especially the things on which the writer can work; and
- closing with the hope that a resolution might be reached, rather than caving in merely to avoid conflict.

Like anything new, this approach to conflict resolution takes time to learn. A couple might wish to start by practicing during times of minimal conflict. Although the letter and material above focuses on couples, the letter-writing process may be just as effective and important when parents want to change the interactions they have with their children.

Letters as Keepsakes of the Heart

Dear Ali,

Today, you played the violin for the first time in front of a large audience. You have played many times for your mother and me and for other family members, especially grandma and grandpa. Since you were 5 years old, you have practiced and played and developed your talent. Today, when you played, I got to watch my little girl share with the world the joy and happiness you bring to music.

I watched your eyes close from time to time. I watched you cradle the violin and move the bow as if both were extensions of your hands. And mostly, I watched you having fun, enjoying the sound of your instrument and the beauty of the music. This is what I have always hoped would happen for you. It is much more important than the fact that you also played so well.

I am proud of you. I am proud of what you have achieved. I feel myself releasing you to the world where you have always belonged. Thank you for letting me be your father.

Love, Dad

This is a letter to mark a special moment. These are words that might get lost or be impossible to share at the close of a ceremony when lots of people or other family members are around. In addition, even if the words could be said, a letter has a greater permanence than memory. It can become a keepsake to warm a child's heart for years to come.

The achievement of change in couple and family counseling is often quite difficult. The experience of having been through a lot together requires something that celebrates and notes the importance of what has come to pass. What does the couple want to say to each other about a new start to their relationship? Where does each family member stand with every other family member now? What do they want to remember about their therapy experience for years to come? What does it mean for them to have made a difference in each other's lives? For what are they thankful? What hopes and dreams are now real and possible? Like the letter above from a father to his daughter, a letter at significant moments in couple or family therapy can mark change as growth, as both welcome and essential.

Letters as Therapeutic Markers

White and Epston (1990; Epston & White, 1992) have been exemplary in using of letters in therapy. Their use of letters may have started as a matter of convenience, a means of summarizing notes from a session, but letters as therapy stem from a belief that human experience is rendered in stories. Letters are a way of marking a part of that story as significant; they are a means of both conveying the meaning of a therapeutic experience and stimulating further therapeutic considerations or movement.

White and Epston use letters for various purposes. The ones they send to clients at the end of a session most often note what understandings the person, couple, or family reached in interaction with the counselor. These letters organize what are often multiple meanings presented during therapy, and they serve as both case notes for the counselor and a clarification of the "story" for the client or clients. In addition, letters often arrive at their destination a number of days later, so they have the effect of suggesting that the counselor is thinking about the client during the week and is interested in the client's thinking about issues raised in therapy. Counselors often think of new options or different perspectives after a session is over. Sometimes, therefore, these letters end with or merely present an idea or question that has come to the counselor's mind after the couple or family has left. The question may involve possibilities for clients while they are away or may invite comment or material for the next session.

White and Epston (1990) also use letters

- to challenge prevailing and discouraging parts of people's life stories,
- to develop support for new or "re-authored" stories,
- to mark special events in peoples' lives,
- to recruit clients as experts who might also help others with similar problems, and
- to create certificates of achievement to celebrate special achievements.

These therapeutic uses of letters serve to bridge the gap between the counseling session and the everyday life of clients. The letters extend contact beyond the boundaries of the office and allow couples or families to reflect on meanings that may have otherwise been lost in the process of interacting. Words tend to be spoken once; they land or they are lost. Letters can be read and reread, with different or renewed meanings possible each time. Furthermore, a compilation of letters marks the journey a couple or family takes and may serve as an anchor in future storms, a reminder of strengths and possibilities so important to relapse prevention (Carlson, Sperry, & Lewis, 1997).

Dear Joe and Mary,

I wanted to write and tell you how impressed I am with the risks you've taken in recent weeks and the amazing progress you've made. I really appreciate the commitment both of you have made to this process, and I was pleased when I heard you talk about how your relationship has grown. I'm wondering, as you continue to work hard to build the kind of partnership you both want, what you think your relationship will look like a year from now. If I visited with you two a year from now, what additional changes do you think I would see because of your hard work? Perhaps we can talk about this the next time we meet.

See you then, Jim.

Conclusion

This chapter has provided examples and discussion of several "letters for a change." Whether used to help couples and families enrich or improve their relationships or to enrich the counseling process between sessions, letter writing can be a powerful tool. The reflective experience needed to develop these letters can be beneficial for clients and counselors alike.

References

Becvar, D. S., & Becvar, R. J. (1996). *Family therapy: A systemic integration* (3rd ed.). Boston: Allyn & Bacon.

Bitter, J., & Corey, G. (2001). Family systems therapy. In G. Corey (Ed.), *Theory and practice of counseling and psychotherapy* (6th ed., pp. 382–453). Belmont, CA: Brooks/Cole.

Carlson, J., Sperry, L., & Lewis, J. (1997). *Family therapy: Insuring treatment efficacy*. Pacific Grove, CA: Brooks/Cole.

Epston, D., & White, M. (1992). *Experience, contradiction, narrative & imagination: Selected papers of David Epston & Michael White (1989-1991)*. Adelaide, South Australia: Dulwich Centre Publications.

Gazda, G. M., Asbury, F. R., Balzer, F. J., Childers, W. C., Phelps, R. E., & Walters, R. P. (1999). *Human relations development: A manual for educators* (6th ed.). Boston: Allyn & Bacon.

Greenberg, L. S., & Johnson, S. M. (1988). *Emotionally-focused therapy for couples*. New York: Guilford Press.

Horne, A. M., & Passmore, J. L. (Eds.). (1996). *Family counseling and therapy* (2nd ed.). Itasca, IL: F. E. Peacock.

Nichols, M. P., & Schwartz, R. C. (1998). *Family therapy: Concepts and methods* (4th ed.). Boston: Allyn & Bacon.

White, M., & Epston, D. (1990). *Narrative means to therapeutic ends*. New York: Norton.

■ ■ ■

2

Therapeutic Correspondence: Writing to Make a Point With Notes and Letters

Richard J. Riordan, PhD and Johanna E. Soet, MA

Family counselors are extending work with their clients beyond the counseling hour. The demand for brief therapy and new techniques and an emphasis on the working alliance between clients and counselor are some of the reasons for this new focus. Adjuncts such as support groups (Riordan & Walsh, 1994), spiritual organizations (Riordan & Snow, 1995), and different types of homework (L'Abate, 1992) are now commonly used in counseling. Client reading and client writing done between sessions, called *bibliotherapy* and *scriptotherapy*, respectively, are also becoming popular adjuncts for counselors (Riordan, 1996). In this chapter, we describe one form of scriptotherapy—therapeutic correspondence—that can be useful when selectively applied in couples and family counseling. This technique differs from other forms of scriptotherapy in that the counselor is mainly responsible for the written communication, although clients may take part in the writing process.

Forms of Therapeutic Correspondence

Therapeutic correspondence may take many forms. Our main interest in this chapter is in the use of therapeutic correspondence, mainly by the counselor, as an occasional and selective adjunctive tool between sessions in counseling with couples and families. Riordan and Ketchum (1996) outlined 10 (among many other) possible ways to use therapeutic correspondence: (a) to engage people who are reluctant to come to counseling; (b) to clarify, request, or make a suggestion; (c) to emphasize something discovered in session; (d) to describe postsession thoughts; (e) to intervene with stuck clients to help resolve their concerns; (f) to congratulate clients for successfully tackling problems; (g) to acknowledge clients' unique histories of struggle and identify alternative narratives; (h) to provoke clients to foster movement; (i) to predict positive future outcome of clients' efforts in counseling; and (j) to provide encouragement, reinforcement, and closure at termination. Exhibit 2.1 provides example sentences for each of these types of letters.

Theoretical Underpinnings

Therapeutic correspondence, like all forms of scriptotherapy, is a pantheoretical technique that may be integrated into any approach. Theoretical support for scriptotherapy is derived from many sources. Using a psychosomatic theory of inhibition, Buck (1984) and Pennebaker (1990) suggest that writing releases clients from the debilitating work of repressing traumatic and troubling thoughts and feelings. This decreases stress on the autonomic nervous system, which may lead to better health. The benefits of scriptotherapy can also be understood using general learning theory, in which practice and physical activity are considered critical factors in knowledge and skill acquisition (L'Abate, 1992). The physical aspect of writing can assist clients in participating actively in practicing the desired thinking skills. However, when discussing therapeutic correspondence where the counselor may be the primary writer, research in human communication and change is particularly relevant. For example, Watzlawick, Weakland, and Fisch (1974) noted that rigid patterns of ineffective interaction may be altered by changing some aspect of the event. A shift from talking to writing may allow the interacting parties to reframe the situation, thus generating different perceptions, expectations, and behavior.

The differences between writing and talking as modalities of intervention in counseling have drawn considerable attention in the literature in recent years (L'Abate, 1992). Contrasts between the two modalities can account for the unique appeal of both. Each modality is subject to different rules of communication. In face-to-face communication, for instance, nonverbal communication such as facial expressions, inappropriate smiles, and fluttering eyes can add important nuances to the interaction and frequently change the entire meaning of an utterance. A counselor can listen for inflections, changes in pronunciation, stuttering, or nervous laughter. Verbal exchanges are more negotiable transactions. That is, if you say something wrong, you can immediately retract it, change it, apologize, or claim to be kidding. During a face-to-face encounter, one can clarify or cancel utterances immediately while listening and looking at the effect they are having on the clients.

Writing has none of the aforementioned features unless the writer painstakingly and graphically incorporates them into the page (e.g., as fiction writers do). Even then, writing is not retractable and is usually one-way communication. Nevertheless, these fundamental differences between face-to-face and written communication are what recommend each as having its own unique appeal as a therapeutic tool. Each modality has its special purposes to be chosen as efficiency or other tactical purposes suggest. Thus, writing may provide an alternate means of communication that can allow a counselor to selectively address issues in a different way or in ways that reinforce what is being done in session.

Recent use of therapeutic correspondence has been strongly influenced by the narrative and solution-focused therapies (Nunnally & Lipchick, 1989; Wojcik & Iverson, 1989). For example, White and Epston (1990), in outlining the usefulness of writing in counseling, have argued that Western society is ocularcentric: It often privileges what is seen over what is heard. Using this cultural value, written communication can more dramatically formalize and legitimize the knowledge, authority, and experience of the clients. In order to perceive change or the possibility of change, clients can be enabled to plot the sequences of life events through time. Writing can thus facilitate the mapping of clients' experiences onto the temporal dimension. This frees them to author and re-author their experiences at the same time that more constructive and mentally sound approaches to life are being incorporated through counseling. White and Epston suggested that writing frees clients' short-term memory, allowing for an expansion of information that can be processed.

Logistical Underpinnings

Because therapeutic letter writing traditionally has not been used in counseling, little has been written to assist the practitioner in using the technique. White and Epston's (1990) *Narrative Means to Therapeutic Ends* is an excellent reference for those wishing to explore in depth the possible uses of therapeutic correspondence with couples and families. The authors' descriptions of family dynamics and interventions made in letters and notes and the rewriting of personal, couple, and family narratives provide a comprehensive and elaborate picture of the technique. Whereas the book may give the reader the impression that letter writing is to be used extensively and frequently, our experience suggests that counselors are unlikely to do intensive letter writing. If for no other practical reason, letter writing probably is unacceptable as billable time. Moreover, counselors must keep in mind that clients do not come to counseling to write or be written to. They come to talk and to experience spontaneity in both the give and take. Thus, literature reports of counseling through written correspondence serve to remind us of the special power of the written word, as reminders of alternatives, options, and tools available for doing good counseling.

Riordan and Ketchum (1996), on the other hand, outlined some limits and practical recommendations for using therapeutic correspondence as an adjunct to face-to-face counseling. First, because letter writing in counseling may be a new skill for the practitioner, it should be practiced on a trial basis. The notion that writing may be helpful in counseling should be discussed with clients in the first session, and it is especially important to explore thoroughly issues of confidentiality. Depending on the mode of communication, the likelihood of someone other than the clients opening a letter, the identification of the return address, or concerns about electronic mail access are some of the issues that should be addressed. Moreover, the written word tends to carry a lot of weight, so written communications with clients should mainly be encouraging and err on the positive side. Negative communications stand a chance of being received poorly and should be reserved for sessions. Riordan and Ketchum (1996) recommended offering clients an opportunity to reciprocate in sending notes or letters. Some clients may be particularly able and willing to communicate in special and additive ways through writing.

Other logistical issues ought to be considered when working with couples and families. For example, correspondence should be addressed to the couple or to all members in the family, not one member only. Singling out a member of the family may have the undesirable effect of placing the counselor in alliance with one family member to the exclusion of the others. When a letter is written to a couple or family, they should be encouraged to read the letter together before processing the content of the correspondence. White and Epston (1990) described instances where the counselor composes a letter with an individual or family to a missing member. In such cases, careful attention should be paid to the input of family members, and only content that is agreed on by all should be included.

Advantages and Disadvantages

Like any therapeutic technique, the use of therapeutic correspondence has advantages and disadvantages. The advantages include the permanence and strength of the written word. Combined with face-to-face interaction, written communication can serve to reinforce and enhance the message the counselor is trying to get across. When focused on the positive, therapeutic correspondence may improve the working alliance, perhaps signaling a special commitment on the part of the counselor. Finally, a written note between sessions may extend the impact of the individual sessions into clients' daily lives, encouraging them to continue their work between counseling sessions.

The disadvantages of therapeutic correspondence include the possibility of fostering unnecessary dependence by introducing between-session contact between counselor and clients, thereby expanding the boundaries of the relationship. Moreover, even when security and confidentiality issues are discussed thoroughly, there is still a potential for compromising the security of the written exchange. Such an event could be distressing to both clients and the counselor. In addition, because therapeutic correspondence is not a skill routinely taught to counselors-in-training, careful consideration and effort must be given to learning and practicing the technique. Implementation may also require time beyond that normally given to clients. Finally, there is a dearth of empirical research to guide clinicians on the optimal use of this technique, even though the increasing number of anecdotal reports supporting it are most encouraging.

Conclusion

Through selective writing of therapeutic correspondence in couples and family work, counselors can access ways of influencing counseling that have the potential of supplementing session interventions. The power of the written word and its known differences from verbal interactions, however, require that counselors be thoughtful and primarily affirmative in their renditions of written interventions. Nonetheless, the power of the written word may be harnessed in ways that may go beyond what can be easily accomplished in sessions.

References

Buck, R. (1984). *Communication of emotion.* New York: Guilford Press.

L'Abate, L. (1992). *Programmed writing: A paratherapeutic approach for intervention with individuals, couples and families.* Pacific Grove, CA: Brooks/Cole.

Nunnally, E., & Lipchick, E. (1989). Some use of writing in solution focused brief therapy. *Journal of Independent Social Work, 4,* 5–19.

Pennebaker, J. W. (1990). *Opening up: The healing power of confiding in others.* New York: Avon Books.

Riordan, R. J. (1996). Scriptotherapy: Therapeutic writing as a counseling adjunct. *The Journal of Counseling and Development, 74,* 263–269.

Riordan, R. J., & Ketchum, S. B. (1996). Therapeutic correspondence: The usefulness of notes and letters in counseling. *Georgia Journal of Professional Counseling, 4,* 31–40.

Riordan, R. J., & Snow, M. (1995). Spirituality: Some practical points for counselors. *Georgia Journal of Mental Health Counseling, 2,* 10–19.

Riordan, R. J., & Walsh, L. (1994). Guidelines for professional referral to A. A. and other twelve–step groups. *Journal of Counseling and Development, 72,* 351–355.

Watzlawick, P., Weakland, J. H., & Fisch, R. (1974). *Change: Principles of problem formation and problem resolution.* New York: Norton.

White, M., & Epston, D. (1990). *Narrative means to therapeutic ends.* New York: Norton.

Wojcik, J. V., & Iverson, E. R. (1989). Therapeutic letters: The power of the printed word. *Journal of Strategic and Systematic Therapies, 8,* 77–81.

■ ■ ■

EXHIBIT 2.1
Therapeutic Uses of Letters and Notes: Some Examples

1. Invitation	"Your wife and I both feel that your presence in therapy with us would strengthen the work we are doing."
2. Clarification request	"I would like you to rent the movie *Ordinary People* and view it together before our next session."
3. Discovery	"Now that you know that about each other it should help you to review your commitment to further exploration."
4. Postsession thoughts	"As I thought about what we did last week, I was even more convinced we have made a break-through."
5. Intervention	"It will help if you all read the enclosed handout on verbal abuse before the next session."
6. Congratulations	"You two can be proud of the hard work you have done in therapy. You deserve the progress you are making."
7. Acknowledgment of unique struggle	"I would like to remind you that you are in an unusual situation. It may be helpful to think of how your deceased parents would be proud of the way you are handling it."
8. Provocation	"I'm not sure the two of you can refrain from your destructive negative language for a whole week."
9. Prediction	"If the work the two of you have done continues as it has, you will feel like you have gotten new lives."
10. Closure	"You should to be proud of the way you have learned to handle adversity on your own. My best wishes go with you."

3

Split Team Therapy

Brian S. Canfield, EdD

Split team therapy (STT) is a team approach to counseling that conceptualizes the therapy process as an interplay between client, counselor, and a supervision team. The approach is a variation of the reflecting team approach used by a number of family therapy clinicians (Brock & Barnard, 1988; Watzlawick & Coyne, 1980) and pioneered by members of the Milan Family Institute. In the treatment team approach, the counselor and supervision team play roles of expert and co-creator with the constantly changing family system (Friedlander, Wildman, & Heatherington, 1991). However, unlike the traditional reflecting team approach, STT is a collaborative process and minimizes the hierarchical nature of therapy. The client, counselor, and supervision team are co-laborers in the same therapy unit, working to the same end.

Conceptually, STT divides the treatment system into three separate subsystems: the client subsystem, the therapist subsystem, and the supervision team subsystem. However, these divisions are arbitrary and fluid, and the physical location of subsystem members may shift at various points in the therapy process. Supervision team members may join the therapy session, and a member of the client family may be asked to join the supervision team in the observation room in order to gain or generate differing perspectives that may benefit the therapy process.

STT takes advantage of the differences that typically exist among family members over a particular issue. At times, members of the therapy or supervision team subsystems may adopt the perspective of a member, or members, of the client subsystem in order to assist in the therapy process. All elements of the larger treatment system work together to the same end, that of assisting the client in attaining the goals of therapy.

Therapy System

As previously noted, in STT the treatment system is divided into three separate subsystems. The *client subsystem* typically consists of the symptom bearer or identified patient and the complainant. The client may be both symptom bearer and complainant, or the "symptoms" and complaints may be expressed by several persons such as a couple, nuclear family, or extended family unit. The *therapist subsystem* refers to the person or persons who work primarily in the therapy room with the client. This subsystem may involve a single counselor or a team. The *supervision team subsystem* refers to the supervisor or colleagues who work primarily in a consultative capacity. However, the distinction between the counselor and the supervision team is largely arbitrary, and the functional roles of both often shift during the course of treatment.

Therapy Setting

Use of a split team approach requires clinic facilities that contain an observation room in close proximity to the therapy room. Ideally, the observation room is adjacent to the therapy room and equipped with a one-way mirror to allow for live viewing of the therapy session. The therapy room and supervision room should be connected with a two-way telephone or intercom system allowing communication between the parties. Alternately, the observation room may be connected to the therapy room through a live-feed closed-circuit video camera and monitor system, with telephone or intercom connection.

In clinical settings that lack an observation room with a video system, observation mirror, or two-way telephone hookup, the supervision team may occupy the therapy room along with the counselor and client, provided the therapy room is large enough to accommodate them all. However, this configuration limits the split team approach and should only be used as a last resort when other, more suitable facilities are unavailable.

A therapy session typically begins with the client and counselor in the therapy room and the supervision team in the adjacent observation room. At any point, however, the physical location of individuals may change. The counselor may go to the observation room for consultation; the supervision team, or representatives of the team, may enter the therapy room to confer with the counselor and client; or the client (or members of the client system) may be invited into the observation room to consult with the supervision team or observe the interactions of other family members with the counselor. Such decisions are collaborative, with administrative authority residing with the counselor and supervisor.

Theoretical Foundations

STT lends itself to a variety of family therapy theoretical orientations including structural, strategic, communication, and family of origin therapies. STT has broad utility with therapies that may be characterized as stemming from modernist philosophy as well as to those theoretical approaches of family therapy that stem from postmodern perspectives.

STT operates from a belief that most client problems are embedded in patterns of human interaction and that these behavioral patterns are largely maintained by client perceptions. STT provides a therapeutic context in which client perceptions may be challenged and altered, often in creative ways unavailable in traditional dyadic therapies. As the client becomes aware of various perspectives offered by the counselor and team, perceptions and behaviors shift. As Becvar, Canfield, and Becvar (1997) stated, clients may find it possible to make a perceptual shift to a different perspective, one in which the problem is no longer viewed as a problem or the essence of the problem is changed. Facilitating this shift requires that clients be offered differing perspectives that challenge clients' established perceptions and interpretations.

The split team approach views therapy as a collaborative process in which the role of the counselor and supervision team is consultative and the client, counselor, and team engage in meaningful conversations about an issue. This approach is in contrast to individual approaches involving a single client and a single therapist. In individual approaches, the counselor to some extent must agree with the client, disagree with the client, or avoid stating a perspective. Although the relative degree of "agreement" or "disagreement" may vary, only three relational positions exist with regard to beliefs on any particular issue.

In the first relational position, the counselor and client are in agreement and share a common perspective. In this position the client may feel a high level of support from the counselor. However, the counselor cannot challenge the client's perspective or beliefs without risking, to some degree, conflict and possible alienation from the client. Moreover, whereas the client–counselor "agreement" may build consensus and a sense of support, it maintains the status quo and does little to challenge unproductive beliefs or offer new perspectives.

In the second relational position, the counselor is in disagreement with the client and offers a different perspective on a particular issue. In this relational position, the counselor and client are to some degree in conflict. Ultimately, one party must yield to the beliefs of the other in order to avoid stagnation. This position underlies the premise held in many individual approaches to therapy in which the client must ultimately discard his or her "flawed" beliefs or perceptions and embrace the "correct perspectives" held by the "expert" therapist. Failure to do so is labeled *resistance* on the part of the client.

The counselor may, by virtue of expert position or persuasive logic, change the client's perspective. However, such a relational position forces an intellectual power play and poses a risk to therapy when the client does not accept the differing perspective offered by the counselor. When that happens, the counselor may lose credibility with the client. In some cases, a client may elect to terminate therapy, believing that the counselor's expression of disagreement implies lack of understanding or lack of acceptance of the client's beliefs. The counselor's stated disagreement with the client's belief may be viewed as an attempt to "control" the client.

From a constructivist perspective, however, the subjective merit of a particular belief does not matter as much as the client's ownership of that belief. Although it is certainly appropriate and necessary for the counselor to create an environment that allows existing client beliefs to be challenged, the counselor's relative position of agreement or disagreement with the client on a given issue does not necessarily facilitate perceptual change and may actually impede the process.

STT provides an alternate approach to therapy that avoids many of the potential problems of direct client–counselor agreement or disagreement on any given issue. The use of the split team expands the communication process of therapy and greatly increases the number of perspectives available to the client. As a therapeutic resource, the therapy team (consisting of the counselor and supervision team) "controls" two of the possible perspectives available to the client. These particular perspectives may be created and manipulated in order to assist the therapy process. This allows a number of potentially useful therapeutic alliances or therapeutic splits to be created and dissolved, as needed, to assist the client and the therapy process. Furthermore, each of the possible relational positions of agreement or disagreement, as stated by either the counselor or supervision team, vary on a continuum from marginal to absolute agreement or disagreement, creating an infinite number of possible relational positions with the client.

Creating a therapeutic alliance with the client through voicing agreement on a particular issue has been noted by several family therapy clinicians and theorists as an effective technique of family therapy (Breit, Im, & Wilner, 1983; Sherman & Fredman, 1986; Watzlawick & Coyne, 1980; Watzlawick, Weakland, & Fisch, 1974). The primary object of creating a therapeutic alliance is to support one or more members of the client subsystem in making desired changes by stating agreement with member perspective on a particular issue.

Whereas the creation of a therapeutic alliance is an important element of STT, the creation of a therapeutic split is used with equal frequency. The counselor or the supervision team (or both) may agree (ally) or disagree (split) with various members of the client system as a tactical maneuver of therapy.

When members of the client subsystem agree on a particular issue, there are nine primary relational possibilities among the client, counselor, and supervision team:

1. The counselor and supervision team agree with each other and with the client's perspective.
2. The counselor and supervision team agree with each other and disagree with the client's perspective.
3. The counselor and supervision team disagree with each other. The counselor agrees with the client, whereas the supervision team disagrees with the client.
4. The counselor and supervision team disagree with each other. The supervision team agrees with the client, whereas the counselor disagrees with the client.

5. The counselor agrees with the client, whereas the supervision team expresses a lack of adequate information and is therefore unable to offer a perspective at that time.
6. The counselor disagrees with the client, whereas the supervision team expresses a lack of adequate information and is therefore unable to offer a perspective at that time.
7. The supervision team agrees with the client, whereas the counselor expresses a lack of adequate information and is therefore unable to offer a perspective at that time.
8. The supervision team disagrees with the client, whereas the counselor expresses a lack of adequate information and is therefore unable to offer a perspective at that time.
9. The supervision team and the counselor both reflect a lack of adequate information and are therefore unable to offer a perspective at that time.

As a practical consideration, members of a client family system (e.g., Mom, Dad, Son, Daughter) rarely hold identical perspectives on a particular issue. Thus, there are a multitude of possible combinations of therapeutic alliances and splits that may emerge or that may be therapeutically created among various members of the client subsystem, therapist subsystem, and supervision team subsystem. For example, in a case in which Dad and Mom are in opposition over an issue of discipline, the counselor may hold a marginal or neutral agreement with Dad's discipline attempts, whereas the supervision team may express strong disagreement with Dad and support of Mom. This has the effect of allowing both parents to feel support and thus minimizes the possibility that either Dad or Mom may sabotage the therapy process by dropping out.

This creation of "split" support is particularly useful in situations where a client, or a member of the client system, consistently expresses general opposition to the counselors as "experts." By adopting opposite perspectives on an issue in which one set of experts (e.g., the supervision team) voices agreement with the client and another expert (e.g., the counselor) voices disagreement, a therapeutic "double bind" is created in which the client is logically compelled to agree with a perspective held by one of the treatment subsystems. The consequence of such an agreement is to remove both the counselor and supervision team from the expert role and to create an alliance between the client previously perceived as oppositional and either the counselor or the supervision team.

Furthermore, the creation of a therapeutic alliance (or therapeutic split) is limited to a particular issue at a particular time in the therapy process. The perspective held by the counseling or supervision subsystems may change in its intensity or even be contradicted and reversed in order to assist the client in gaining a new perspective on the issue at hand. The logical justification for the counselor's or supervision team's shift in perspective may be attributed to acquisition of new information from the client or to the client having persuaded or convinced the counselor (or supervision team) that its previously held perspective was flawed. For example, in a case in which Mom is criticized by Dad because of her lack of effective discipline with a child, and where the team was previously supportive of Dad, the supervision team may shift its alliance from Dad over to Mom by stating the following:

> "The team wishes to change its position about the lack of discipline in the household. Her efforts in recent weeks have convinced the team that Mom has indeed tried everything reasonably possible. Perhaps what's needed is the help of an additional person rather than a change in Mom's efforts."

This shift in perspective on the part of the supervision team (or counselor) also has a modeling effect in that it provides the client with a greater level of comfort and invites a shift in the client's perspective (e.g., "if the 'experts' can change their minds, perhaps its OK for me to change my mind").

The counselor may use the team to emphasize a particular point or perspective in contrast to that held by the client, with the benefit of avoiding direct confrontation with the client. For example, the counselor may say the following to the client:

> "I tend to agree with your view that your son's problem is connected to a lack of teacher responsiveness. However, the team strongly disagrees with you and me. They believe the problem is not so much a school problem as it is a family problem because you and your husband are not getting along very well."

Conclusion

STT has been successfully used with a wide range of clients in clinical settings. The approach focuses on the establishment and shifting of therapeutic alliances and splits in order to illuminate new or differing perceptions on a variety of clinical issues. The approach is collaborative and allows the treatment process to present specific perspectives on therapeutic issues while avoiding the creation of perceptual discrepancies that might otherwise emerge between the client or clients and counselor.

References

Becvar, R., Canfield, B., & Becvar, D. (1997). *Group work: Cybernetic, constructivist, and social constructionist perspectives.* Denver, CO: Love Publishing.

Breit, M. M., Im, W. G., & Wilner, S. (1983). Strategic approaches with resistant families. *American Journal of Family Therapy, 11,* 51–58.

Brock, G., & Barnard, C. (1988). *Procedures in family therapy.* Boston: Allyn & Bacon.

Friedlander, M. L, Wildman, J., & Heatherington, L. (1991). Interpersonal control in structural and Milan systemic family therapy. *Journal of Marital and Family Therapy, 17,* 395–408.

Sherman, R., & Fredman, N. (1986). *Handbook of structured techniques in marriage and family therapy.* New York: Brunner/Mazel.

Watzlawick, P., & Coyne, J. C. (1980). Depression following stroke: Brief, problem–focused family treatment. *Family Process, 19,* 13–18.

Watzlawick, P., Weakland, J. H., & Fisch, R. (1974). *Change: Principles of problem formation and problem resolution.* New York: Norton.

■ ■ ■

4

Using Imaginary Team Members in Couples Counseling

Richard E. Watts, PhD

Often when immersed in a difficult situation, we selectively attend only to the "problem" and ignore alternative perspectives that might help develop solutions. However, when we are able to step out of or step away from difficulties and reflect on the situation, new and preferred meanings are often more readily generated. This idea of stepping out or stepping away in order to create a place for reflection is also useful for helping clients in couples counseling develop preferred perspectives (West, Watts, Trepal, Wester, & Lewis, in press).

The postmodern counseling literature contains numerous interventions that may help to create a neutral place for client reflection; for example, the miracle question and looking for exceptions (Walter & Peller, 1992), externalizing problems and considering unique outcomes (White & Epston, 1990), or using questions to facilitate reflective (Andersen, 1991) or reflexive (Tomm, 1987) thinking, to name a few.

Andersen (1991) suggested the use of "reflecting teams" for helping clients become more reflective in their thinking. In Andersen's original format, reflecting team members discuss their perspectives regarding a particular session in the presence of clients rather than remaining hidden behind the one-way mirror. Clients then discuss their reflections of the reflecting team's conversation. I present a technique loosely based on Andersen's reflective team approach.

According to Freedman and Combs (1996), reflecting teams may comprise persons not actually present in the counseling session. Thus, partners are asked by the counselor to mentally "invite in" one or more persons they respect—individual partners or couples—to serve as team members for creating reflective thinking. These team members may be invited to current and future sessions to help couples create alternative meanings and behaviors.

To begin using the imaginary team approach, the counselor asks the couple to do the following: "Think of one or more persons you respect in the relational role of wife, husband, or partner." The counselor and couple then create a list of team members. To enhance the team member imagery, the counselor might choose to provide chairs for each team member, similar to the use of an empty chair in Gestalt therapy. Counselors may put name tags on the chairs for identification purposes.

After the team is created, the counselor may call on team members for assistance by asking clients questions such as the following:

- What might [he/she/they] say is something that you obviously appreciate about your partner? What might [he/she/they] say your partner experiences when the problem attacks your relationship? [internalized other questions]
- Suppose you are talking to this person or couple in the future after you have made significant progress in your relationship. What changes will [he/she/they] say are evident? What, specifically, will [he/she/they] say is different about your relationship? What specific steps would [he/she/they] identify that you two took to get your relationships to this significant point of change? [future questions]
- What suggestions might [he/she/they] have for responding constructively to the problem? [suggestion question]
- What might [he/she/they] say that you do when anger attacks your partner? [externalizing question]
- What would [he/she/they] say is different about how you two interact when the problem is not a problem? [exception question]
- How would [he/she/they] describe your relationship when you two are relating in ways that you prefer? [unique outcome question]

Follow-up questions for exception and unique outcome questions:

- How would [he/she/they] explain your ability to accomplish such great relational success? [accomplishment or coping question]
- How will [he/she/they] know when you two are starting to move in the direction you both want to go as a couple? [initial movement question]

Numerous questions derived from postmodern approaches (and others) are useful in engaging imaginary team members. Imaginary team members may be excused at any time to allow the couple and counselor to reflect on the team's comments. Team members may be invited to return later in the session or during any future session to assist in the reflection process.

Inviting imaginary team members into sessions is a very flexible technique. Team members are selected by the couple, they may be called on for assistance at any time in the counseling process, and any number of questions or interventions many be used. The technique may help couples and counselors engage in the kind of reflective thinking that serves to assist in creating preferred alternative perspectives in counseling.

References

Andersen, T. (Ed.). (1991). *The reflecting team: Dialogues and dialogues about the dialogues.* New York: Norton.

Freedman, J., & Combs, G. (1996). *Narrative therapy: The social construction of preferred realities.* New York: Norton.

Tomm, K. (1987). Interventive interviewing: Part II. Reflexive questioning as a means to enable self-healing. *Family Process, 26,* 167-183.

Walter, J. L., & Peller, J. E. (1992). *Becoming solution-focused in brief therapy.* New York: Brunner/Mazel.

West, J. D., Watts, R. E., Trepal, H. C., Wester, K. L., & Lewis, T. F. (in press). Opening space for client reflection: A postmodern consideration. *The Family Journal.*

White, M., & Epston, D. (1990). *Narrative means to therapeutic ends.* New York: Norton.

■ ■ ■

5

Conveying the "Not Knowing" Position in Marriage and Family Counseling

Phyllis Erdman, PhD

Early in their training, counselors learn the interpersonal skills requisite to provide a trusting, nonjudgmental environment where clients feel safe to share their personal stories (Egan, 1990). Helping skills such as unconditional positive regard, genuineness and congruence, and empathy are part of a joining process and have been described as the necessary conditions for client development (Rogers, 1958). Minuchin and Fishman (1981) described *joining* as the process whereby family members know they are accepted and understood. They suggest that joining is "more of an attitude than a technique" (p. 31). Weingarten (1992) expanded this concept by introducing the term *intimacy* into counselor–client relationships. As she described it, *intimacy* refers to the quality of interaction between counselors and clients that goes beyond expressing feelings of warmth and closeness toward the client. Intimate interactions are those in which counselors and clients co-create meanings and are considered more therapeutic than nonintimate interactions, in which the meaning is provided by counselors for clients.

The concept of co-creating meaning is found in social constructionist approaches to counseling (Bischoff & McKeel, 1993; Bischoff,

McKeel, Moon, & Sprenkle, 1996; Bobele, Gardner, & Biever, 1995; Duncan, Solovey, & Rusk, 1992; Freedman & Combs, 1996; Shilts, Filippino, & Nau, 1994; Weingarten, 1992; White & Epston, 1990). These approaches share the following common tenets:

- realities are socially constructed,
- realities are constituted through language,
- realities are organized and maintained through narrative, and
- there are no essential truths. (Freedman & Combs, 1996, p. 22)

Clients' views of reality, and how they see problems, become paramount to the therapeutic process and serve to identify the points where change is most likely to occur (Duncan et al., 1992). An important task in counseling is for clients and counselors to collaborate on their perceptions of the problem and the solution so that counseling becomes more client-driven than counselor-driven (Bischoff & McKeel, 1993; Bischoff et al., 1996; Duncan et al., 1992; Shilts et al., 1994). White and Epston (1990) suggested that when counselors define client problems on the basis of their own expert knowledge, they do not see how the problem is defined by the client, thereby limiting the options for change. The process of counseling should be an attempt to create a context in which collaboration thrives in order to help the client and the counselor co-define the problem and to revise the problem definition if needed (Duncan et al., 1992). According to Schwaber, "our pathway to what is unconscious is more likely to be reached when it is jointly discovered rather than unilaterally inferred, and the yield will be more empirically derived data" (quoted in Weingarten, 1992, p. 45).

This collaborative approach toward counseling shifts the role of the counselor from that of an expert to that of a nonexpert (Bischoff & McKeel, 1993; Bischoff et al., 1996; Duncan et al., 1992; Shilts et al., 1994). Bischoff et al. described a three-stage model that solicits clients' input in order to assess the course of counseling. They indicated that the timing of this intervention is crucial to the process and should be done during the working stages of counseling to be most effective. They also emphasize the importance of counselors maintaining an accepting, nonjudgmental stance so that feedback to clients is perceived as helpful rather than as threatening. Duncan et al. recommended that counselors take a one-down position, but they emphasized that it must be based on a conceptual framework that discredits the belief that there is one true cause of clients' problems.

The technique described in this chapter is based on social constructionism and can only thrive in the context of a safe and nonthreatening therapeutic relationship. It describes a process whereby a counselor engages in a one-down position and solicits feedback from a client in an attempt to verify the client's perception of the problem and to create together new possibilities for change.

Procedure

After video taping a counseling session, the counselor requests that the clients take the tape home and view it, looking specifically for what they consider to be meaningful moments of the session. Examples of meaningful moments are described to clients as the following: (a) something said or done that all family members regarded as important or as new information, (b) something that a family member said and was not acknowledged as important by all other members, (c) observation of nonverbal reactions to family members, or (d) a reaction (i.e., verbal response, body language, shifting the topic) or lack of reaction (i.e., no verbal response, silence, shifting the topic) by the counselor to something said by a family member. This is not an inclusive list; clients may designate anything as meaningful. If family members have the capacity to work together with minimal conflict, they are asked to view the tape as a family. Otherwise, each family member is asked to view it independently.

Family members are asked to mark the place on the tape where the meaningful moments occurred and to bring it back to the next session to share with the counselor and other family members. The counselor then develops questions from these meaningful moments, presents them to family members, and solicits their feedback. Typical examples of the counselor-client discussion about the video might include comments such as the following:

Client: When I told Kathy about what happened, I could just feel Jeff tensing up, but I didn't know how to acknowledge him or what to do.

Counselor: So when you told Kathy about that incident, you really wanted me to ask Jeff what he was feeling because you didn't know how. Is that right?

Client: When I told you what my mother said about it, you never said anything. I got the message that it wasn't important.

Counselor: How could I have let you know that I really did hear what you were saying?

Client: Yeah, Joe and I do argue a lot over Mary's behavior but it's because she reminds me so much of myself when I was her age.

Counselor: So it's not the arguing that seems to be causing you so much pain, it's the memory of your childhood. Maybe we need to talk more about that.

Client: Just look at everyone. I'm the one who is obviously working hard to keep this family together. And everyone else just sits there, and lets me do the work. It's a perfect picture of our lives at home—me against them.

Counselor: I guess I didn't pick up on your feelings of being overwhelmed and sort of used. And also all alone in this thing. What needs to happen in here to make you feel supported?

Impact on the Session

Unless counselors have the luxury of having an observing team (e.g., watching through a one-way mirror) to keep them on target, it is easy to get bombarded with so much information that they lose the focus of the session. Feedback solicited from client reflections has the capacity to shift the overall focus of the session in helpful ways. It is also an effective intervention for engaging nonparticipating family members in the session. Family members who are not participating usually find it more difficult to refuse responding when they perceive the request to come from another family member, rather than from the counselor.

The counselor may also be avoiding certain issues brought up by the client, especially if the counselor is struggling with similar unresolved issues. When the counselor acknowledges the client's feedback on the issues and his or her nonresponse to them, the counselor–client relationship takes on a more genuine and intimate quality.

By taking a one-down position and allowing the client to be the expert on his or her life story, the counselor conveys confidence in the family's strength. It may also serve as a genuine and legitimate plea from the counselor that says, "Help me to help you. Tell me what else I need to know to help each of you move forward."

Contraindications

This technique is most effective after at least three or four sessions. If attempted too early, clients may view it as less genuine and as being based more on counselor incompetence. The counselor–client relationship requires time to develop so that such openness is perceived positively by the client.

Some clients may abuse the opportunity for feedback by using it to avoid areas they do not want to address or to exert control over the session. Counselors should be aware of such attempts and confront the client accordingly.

Conclusion

Clients are the true "experts" on their lives. Using the "not knowing" position allows counselors to tap into the expert knowledge that clients possess. By engaging in a one-down position and soliciting feedback from clients, counselors can better understand clients' perceptions of problems and facilitate co-creation of new possibilities for change.

References

Bischoff, R. J., & McKeel, A. J. (1993). Collegial consultations. *Journal of Systemic Therapies, 12*, 50–60.

Bischoff, R. J., McKeel, A. J., Moon, S. M., & Sprenkle, D. H. (1996). Therapist-conducted consultation: Using clients as consultants to their own therapy. *Journal of Marital and Family Therapy, 22*, 359–379.

Bobele, M., Gardner, G., & Biever, J. (1995). Supervision as social construction. *Journal of Systemic Therapies, 14*, 14–25.

Duncan, B. L., Solovey, A. D., & Rusk, G. S. (1992). *Changing the rules: A client-directed approach to therapy.* New York: Guilford Press.

Egan, G. (1990). *The skilled helper.* Pacific Grove, CA: Brooks/Cole.

Freedman, J., & Combs, G. (1996). *Narrative therapy: The social construction of preferred realities.* New York: Norton.

Minuchin, S., & Fishman, H. C. (1981). *Family therapy techniques.* Cambridge, MA: Harvard University Press.

Rogers, C. (1958). The characteristics of a helping relationship. *Personnel and Guidance Journal, 37*, 6–16.

Shilts, L., Filippino, C., & Nau, D. D. (1994). Client-informed therapy. *Journal of Systemic Therapies, 13*, 39–52.

Weingarten, K. (1992). A consideration of intimate and non-intimate interactions in therapy. *Family Process, 31*, 45–59.

White, M., & Epston, D. (1990). *Narrative means to therapeutic ends.* New York: Norton.

■ ■ ■

6

Womanist Interventions: Working With African American Women in Couples and Family Therapy

Marsha Wiggins Frame, PhD and Carmen Braun Williams, PhD

The experiences of African American women are grounded in a culture rich with healing traditions and practices. Themes of communalism, extended kinship ties, emotional expressiveness, ritual, music and dance, and folkloric wisdom are central to African American culture (Jones, 1993; White, 1984). The place of African American women in this cultural legacy is distinctive because of their experience of both racial and gender victimization (Davis, 1983; Giddings, 1996). Therefore, it is imperative for counselors to consider the interrelationship among African American women's experiences with race, gender, community, family, and spirituality. The two interventions discussed below aim at meeting this challenge.

Womanist Themes

Walker (1983) was the first to label the folk culture of Black women, with its commitment to survival and wholeness of self and others, as *womanist*. African American women theologians have expanded the term *womanist* to describe

> Black women's experiences of relation, loss, gain, faith, hope, cel-
> ebration and defiance. . . . Womanist theology challenges all oppres-
> sive forces impeding Black women's struggle for survival and for
> the development of a positive, productive quality of life conducive
> to women's and the family's freedom and well-being. (Williams, 1993,
> p. xiv)

An important task for counselors is "retrieving this often hidden or diminished female tradition of catalytic action" (Williams, 1993, p. 26) and assisting Black women clients to use it for self-agency.

Biblical Stories

Using biblical stories can be particularly effective. Because many African American women have deep roots in the Christian tradi-tion through the Black church, they may be familiar with biblical stories that can provide both authority and inspiration for personal change.

For example, the biblical story of Hagar (Genesis 16:1-6; Genesis 21:9–21) is a powerful metaphor that symbolizes both African Ameri-can women's suffering and survival. Hagar, an Egyptian slave, is portrayed in the biblical text as the solution to the infertility prob-lem that plagued Sarai, wife of the Hebrew patriarch, Abraham. Whereas childlessness meant a loss of status for women in biblical times, Sarai proposed that Hagar, her slave, be a surrogate mother and bear a child by Abraham, thus giving him an heir. Indeed, Hagar becomes a "second wife" for Abraham, and this relationship threat-ens Sarai. As a result of Sarai's treatment of her, Hagar runs away from her mistress, thus becoming "the first woman in the Bible to liberate herself from oppressive power structures" (Williams, 1993, p. 19). Ishmael is born, and Hagar, like many African American women, "goes out into the world to make a living for herself and her son" and triumphs over "surrogacy, motherhood, rape, homelessness, and economic and sexual oppression" (p. 33).

The counselor working with Black women clients who value the Bible may want to ask them to read the biblical account of Hagar's life and ask these and other questions: How is Hagar's story like your story? What are Hagar's strengths and resources, and how are your strengths and resources similar or different from hers? What circumstances in your life continue to enslave you? What kind of liberation or freedom do you need in order to thrive? What is your personal "wilderness" like? Who or what can you count on for support? By helping African American women clients claim the power and the authority of a biblical story and see the ways in which their lives mirror biblical women's lives, counselors may enable them to gain a vision of the life they want and help them overcome the obstacles and challenges that may stand in their way.

Confronting Colorism

A thorny issue for many African Americans is *colorism*, the system of valuation among people of color of intraracial variations in skin tone. African Americans historically have valued lighter skin tones over darker shades of brown skin. Comparisons of siblings on the basis of skin color, statements about a Black child's hair being "good hair" because it is less kinky than a sibling's, and correlations between a child's color and his or her attractiveness or intelligence are typical expressions of colorism in Black families (Boyd-Franklin, 1989).

The counselor must be aware of the enormous pain colorism has caused many African Americans and the anger family members may feel, often not overtly expressed, toward others in the family who perpetuate colorism. With this in mind, the counselor may begin the confronting colorism exercise by asking each family member to draw himself or herself on a large sheet of paper. Because of the myriad of skin colors within many Black families, the counselor must be sure to have a range of colors available for the family to use. After family members have completed their drawings, each member is asked to describe his or her picture. These descriptions might include not only physical but personality traits as well. Both pieces of information are useful. It is important, however, that the counselor specifically ask about physical features (e.g., skin color) if clients omit them. Family members then are asked to identify similarities and differences among one another. Because Black families are often extended, the clients also could be asked to describe other significant family members whose traits are similar or dissimilar to theirs.

Next, the counselor asks all family members to explore their feelings about these characteristics, stating three positive and three negative messages they have received from others about how they look (and how they act). The next step is to ask family members to reveal the source or sources of the messages and how the messages affected them. At this point, it is very important for all family members, adults and children alike, to tell their stories. When children of any age have the opportunity to hear about their parents' parallel struggles with difficult racial issues, and likewise when parents are able to hear their children's pain, deeper understanding of and empathy for one another often is facilitated (Boyd-Franklin, 1989). This part of the exercise may take considerable time, especially if several family members are present. It is critical that counselors allow sufficient time for all family members to share their feelings, even if this requires more than one session.

The last step of the confronting colorism exercise involves creating a family list of affirmations. On large pieces of paper taped to the wall, each person writes his or her name at the top of one of the sheets of paper. Family members then take turns writing a positive statement on each person's sheet. Each statement affirms something about that person's physical appearance. The counselor directs the family toward specific positive affirmations about physical features identified earlier as the target for negative messages. The list also could be extended to include affirmations about personality characteristics. The family is asked to find a place in the house to post their list where everyone can see it. They are asked to read their list and to say at least one positive thing to each other every day during the next week and to report on this at the next session.

Conclusion

Biblical stories and the confronting colorism exercise are only two of potentially numerous counseling interventions based on womanist themes that may be used with African American women. Using the experiences of African American women to facilitate their growth and development is a sensitive and empowering way of working with this marginalized population.

References

Boyd-Franklin, N. (1989). *Black families in therapy: A multisystems approach*. New York: Guilford Press.

Davis, A. Y. (1983). *Women, race, and class*. New York: Random House.

Giddings, P. (1996). *Where and when I enter: The impact of Black women on race and sex in America* (2nd ed.). New York: William Morrow.

Jones, A. E. (1993). *Wade in the water: The wisdom of the spiritual.* Maryknoll, NY: Orbis Books.

Walker, A. (1983). *In search of our mothers' gardens.* New York: Harcourt, Brace, & Jovanovich.

White, J. (1984). *The psychology of Blacks: An Afro-American perspective.* Englewood Cliffs, NJ: Prentice-Hall.

Williams, D. S. (1993). *Sisters in the wilderness: The challenge of womanist God-talk.* Maryknoll, NY: Orbis Books.

■ ■ ■

7

Pad and Pencil Technique

Frank M. Dattilio, PhD

Counselors and therapists who work with couples and families in distress know only too well how arduous such work can be. Couples in distress often submit for treatment with reticence and a great deal of open animosity that, on occasion, makes even the intake a challenge to conduct.

In the course of many years of working with couples in distress, my main focus has been to apply a cognitive–behavioral approach to working with couples and families (Dattilio, 1993, 1994, 1998; Dattilio & Padesky, 1990). The essence of the cognitive–behavioral approach is rooted in restructuring maladaptive thoughts and perceptions and facilitating behavioral change in order to promote healthy and productive interaction among couples or family members.

Cognitive–behavioral techniques have proven to be quite effective because they can be integrated with other treatment modalities (Dattilio, 1993, 1994, 1998; Dattilio & Padesky, 1990). In addition, its efficacy in crisis situations and in the diffusion of intense anger and physical violence is well-documented (e.g., Baucom & Epstein, 1990; Dattilio & Padesky, 1990).

One of the common obstacles that counselors may encounter during their work with couples is the constant interruption by spouses of their partners' attempts to tell their side of a particular situation.

This interruption or intrusion creates an atmosphere of dissension and often inhibits the therapeutic process.

Couple therapists have proposed many interventions for discouraging interruptions by partners. One technique described by Markman, Stanley, and Blumberg (1994) involves providing the partners with one piece of linoleum or another type of floor covering to indicate that the individual who is speaking has the floor and that they are to refrain from interrupting during that time (p. 63). Although this unique technique can be effective with more impulsive clients, it may not work with individuals who interrupt because of a need to disrupt the flow of their partner's conversation. This is especially true during instances when they perceive the content to be inaccurate. Another technique used by Susan Heitler (1995) involves the therapist interrupting the intervening spouse and asking him or her to cease the argument or simply saying "stop." This is often effective but may have to be repeated, taking valuable time away from the therapy process.

More important, couples have indicated that one of the main reasons they spontaneously interrupt their partner is for fear that they will not be able to express their spontaneous thoughts or emotions. Therefore, any technique that allows couples to express their automatic thoughts and their emotional responses without interfering with or interrupting the flow of their partner's narrative may be quite valuable to the therapeutic process.

During a particular case, I noticed a woman fidgeting with a pen she was holding while her husband was giving a rendition of an argument that they had 2 days earlier that led to a physically abusive exchange. Both partners were intent on expressing their rendition. Subjected to hearing her husband's "distorted view of what occurred," the woman became increasingly anxious. As a cognitive–behavior therapist, I wanted very much to ask her what was going through her mind but did not want to interrupt her husband's train of thought. It dawned on me that if she had the opportunity to write down her automatic thoughts and the accompanying emotions, this would be a way for her to direct her attention to a constructive task and at the same time capture the true intensity of her feelings. This would also allow her to feel reassured that she was not losing any of the thought content or emotion and that she could refer to the content when it was her turn. At that point, I suggested that her husband do the same thing. I provided him with a pen and a pad of paper, so that he could capture any thoughts or emotions he had while listening to his wife's rendition of the incident, and he could feel confident that the content would be discussed later.

I was surprised to find that this intervention worked extremely well. The couple expressed satisfaction that none of their thoughts or emotions were left out or ignored. The actual process of the cognitive–behavioral exercise of writing is not only cathartic—it also decreases interruptions and allows spouses to focus their attention and, at the same time, listen to what their partner has to say, keeping written track of valuable information.

This technique is visually displayed in a videotape entitled *Cognitive Therapy With Couples: The Initial Phase of Treatment* (Dattilio, 1996). The technique is effective with couples and may be effectively used with family members during the course of family counseling.

References

Baucom, D. H., & Epstein, N. B. (1990). *Cognitive–behavioral marital therapy.* New York: Brunner/Mazel.

Dattilio, F. M. (1993). Cognitive therapy with couples and families. *The Family Journal, 1,* 51–65.

Dattilio, F. M. (1994). Families in crisis. In F. M. Dattilio & A. Freeman (Eds.), *Cognitive–behavioral strategies in crisis intervention* (pp. 278–301). New York: Guilford Press.

Dattilio, F. M. (1996). *Cognitive therapy with couples: The initial phase of treatment* [Videotape, 56 minutes]. Sarasota, FL: Professional Resource Press.

Dattilio, F. M. (Ed.). (1998). *Case studies in couples and family therapy: Systemic and cognitive perspectives.* New York: Guilford Press.

Dattilio, F. M., & Padesky, C. A. (1990). *Cognitive therapy with couples.* Sarasota, FL: Professional Resource Exchange.

Heitler, S. (1995). *The angry couple. Conflict–focused treatment.* [Videotape, 73 minutes]. New York: Newbridge Professional Programs.

Markman, H. S., Stanley, S., & Blumberg, S. L. (1994). *Fighting for your marriage.* San Francisco: Jossey–Bass.

■ ■ ■

8

Brief Cognitive Couple Therapy: Thoughtful Solutions

Michael L. Baltimore, PhD

Marital and couple therapy is recognized as a specialized area in family therapy and continues to grow as a widely accepted form of clinical practice (Jacobson & Gurman, 1995; Lopez, 1993). Couple therapy is a systems-oriented approach, typically based on an understanding of family therapy theory, system assessment, and family interventions. Presenting issues are understood in the context of the family systems involved, and goals for therapy are identified with the help of the counselor. Whereas many of these systemic models vary depending on their focus on past experiences and intergenerational patterns that currently affect the couple's functioning, other approaches have postmodern underpinnings and concentrate on the couple's current functioning and the here-and-now process issues. Regarding the latter, brief couple therapies have paid particular attention to specific interactions within the sessions and homework assignments between sessions.

One such postmodern approach is solution-focused brief therapy (SFBT; de Shazer, 1991). SFBT espouses a fundamental belief in the individual's ability to solve problems by examining in-place and new solutions, with much less focus on the problem as such. This approach seems applicable to couples conflicts and seems to be widely accepted as a sound therapeutic method.

Another couple therapy model, highly compatible with the solution-focused approach, is cognitive couple therapy (Baucom & Epstein, 1990). This model presents a framework for understanding the types of cognitions used by couples and lends itself to a brief treatment approach. The structure of assessment and intervention used by both solution-focused and cognitive couple therapy can enhance the process of resolving conflict between couples and offers specific techniques to assist couples in reaching their goals. The resulting blended model—combining a cognitive couple therapy model with SFBT—can provide a framework for helping couples.

Cognitive Couple Therapy

Concentration on internal cognitive processes in close relationships has increased in recent years (Lopez, 1993). Baucom and Epstein (1990) have suggested that cognitive variables are natural aspects of the information processing necessary for individuals to understand and evaluate their environments and make decisions about their relationships. Cognitive phenomena are believed to be operating within close relationships to maintain stability or to move toward relationship dysfunction. Several types of cognitive phenomena play important roles in the development and maintenance of relationship functioning: perceptions (what events occur), attributions (why events occur), expectancies (predictions of what will occur), assumptions (the nature of the world and correlation among events), and standards (what "should be"). The therapeutic environment is thus promoted by involving the clients in the understanding of the importance of thought and its connection with behaviors.

Baucom and Epstein (1990) have suggested that these cognitive phenomena are interrelated in their role in relationship dysfunction. They provide information from past and present experiences in order to predict future events and outcomes in close relationships. Baucom and Epstein suggested, however, that perceptions, attributions, expectations, assumptions, and standards are susceptible to distortions and may sometimes be extreme or inaccurate as individuals evaluate their relationships. When one partner's expectations are incongruent with those of the other partner, relationship dissatisfaction is likely to occur. Conversely, when outcomes meet or exceed a partner's expectations, relationship satisfaction is likely to be enhanced. Consequently, individual differences in beliefs regarding relationship outcomes may affect close relationship functioning in significant ways.

Maladaptive cognitions and accompanying behaviors that affect the couple's relationship can be both understood and brought under control by clients. By focusing on automatic thinking, the tendency toward too much attention to the past, and the reinforcement of dysfunctional and repetitive cognitions, the counselor can help introduce appropriate interventions to enhance the couple's relationship.

Description and Use of Cognitions

Understanding cognition in couple relationships is crucial for assessment and selecting appropriate interventions. Paying close attention to how couples use cognitions such as assumptions, expectations, standards, and perceptions is important to structuring interventions. For example, many couples in therapy describe the same situation differently. This happens often in situations of conflict and can lead to argumentative behavior with dire outcomes. Inexperienced counselors may find themselves trying to decide which partner's description is the correct one and can eventually alienate one of the couple or lose the couple altogether.

Relationship cognitions, such as attributions, have been discussed with some frequency in the literature (Baucom & Epstein, 1990; Lopez, 1993). Other relationship cognitions, including expectations and specific beliefs about personal relationships, have received less attention. However, what a person comes to expect in a relationship may predict its outcome and may be a point of entry for the counselor helping a couple. Moreover, lack of consideration for assumptions or other cognitive processes could lead to gaps in relationship assessment.

Solution-Focused Brief Therapy

According to SFBT, clients have already demonstrated success in the couple relationship, but they are not using what works. SFBT focuses on clients' strengths, shifting the time frame to the present, using previous solutions, and addressing what would happen differently if problems miraculously vanished. Attention to solutions and positive interactions is important in helping the couple to begin new, familiar behaviors. One assumption in this model is that even small changes are significant. Crucial to couple work is the assumption that one partner can work on improving the couple relationship. That is, individual couple therapy is valid, because a small change on the part of one person in the relationship can succeed in changing the dyad.

The work of the solution-focused therapist also involves talking about competence. Attention is focused on any gains or progress, both current and from the past, allowing for improved interactions. This basic assumption affirms the belief that people already have solutions to their problems (de Shazer, 1991).

Finally, the miracle question is of no less importance to the solution-focused approach and is asked as follows: "If tomorrow you awoke and all your symptoms (problems, difficulties, etc.) were suddenly gone, what would your life be like?" This seemingly simple question is often quite difficult for clients to answer. It is difficult because individuals have a tendency to become "experts" in their problems. Consequently, a world without the problem is extremely difficult for clients to imagine. The miracle question helps clients to "see" themselves in new situations or circumstances. Skills already possessed by clients are then applied to bring about solutions. Where skills are underdeveloped or nonexistent, the teaching of new skills is appropriate.

Brief Solutions in Cognitive Couple Therapy

The solution-focused approach is a natural accompaniment to the focus on cognitive processes in cognitive couple therapy. Themes from this blended model include the following: doing whatever works (stop doing what does not work); working collaboratively with the client (through their cognitions) such that there is a co-creation of context; shifting the time frame to the present ("Can you tell me about what is happening in your life when things are a little better?"); and helping the client create alternative and more adaptive perceptions of the problem. The counselor helps clients develop or discover cognitions that are solution focused and positive in their effect.

While attending to solutions in this proposed model, attention to both individual and shared beliefs about the couple's relationship is essential. Counselors can facilitate the discovery of solutions for potentially problematic cognitions. For example, perceptions can be diverted from whose view is right to how both partners in the relationship are affected ("Can you imagine that this stress [event, problem, etc.] affects you both?"). Relationship perceptions can have a powerful effect on how a couple attempts to solve the particular problem. Another example, using this same concept of relationship perception, can be illustrated in an in-session intervention. The counselor asks the clients to stand near two separate windows and describe what they see. As they describe their individual views, the counselor points out that neither view is wrong but that both perspectives can be appreciated and respected without arguing about which is right, because in fact they are both right.

The cognitive and solution-focused therapist would also avoid having couples assign blame for their problems. The process, similar to "externalization" in the narrative therapy approach (White & Epston, 1990), attempts to define the problem outside the persons involved. Furthermore, expectations and assumptions about relationship issues are discussed openly with the counselor working to find mutually constructive attributes. Expectations and standards strongly influence relationship outcomes. For example, standards may be placed so high that an individual can never reach them. Unrealistic standards for oneself or one's partner can do serious damage to the relationship. Here the counselor can discuss the expectations the couple had at the start of their relationship: ("Think back to when your relationship began. What were your individual expectations for yourself, and the relationship, at that time?") This question typically allows the couple to detach from the present conflict and recall initial relationship expectations that may still be helpful in the current context.

Finally, setting standards requires reality-based negotiation and discussion. Comparisons considered to be incongruent require careful mediation by the counselor. The counselor may wish to contract with both individuals for slight changes in their behaviors on a selected topic to begin the process of aligning standards with the needs of the partner. Solution-oriented interventions may seem minuscule in proportion to the conflict brought in by a couple. In this model, however, any small change in relationship patterns or interactions may result in larger subsequent changes in the couple's relational functioning. Again, the counselor should be careful to ask when the standards have been met in the recent past in order to keep the focus on solutions in the present. Competence language can be difficult for clients in the midst of conflict, but competencies can be uncovered and used in the therapeutic process. The counselor continues asking specific questions that allow for defining and discussing how competence may be displayed individually or in a dyadic sense. Later in the discussion, the counselor may ask one partner to verify these competencies and describe how he or she manages to accomplish the things that help the relationship.

The process of using cognition with a solution focus helps clients understand that cognitive processes can enhance and support the health of their relationship. The integration of cognitive therapeutic strategies with a solution-focused approach is a natural synthesis of brief therapeutic interventions.

An Applied Framework for Brief Cognitive Couple Therapy

To illustrate the framework for the use of brief cognitive couple therapy, several guidelines are suggested for practitioners.

1. Become familiar with the general cognitive–behavioral approach, which includes teaching clients about their use of cognition in the relationship.
2. Encourage clients to express their initial and current view of cognitions (i.e., perceptions, attributions, expectations, assumptions, and standards). Focus on a single cognition initially.
3. Become familiar with the solution-focused approach. Stay present-oriented and focus on what is working currently. Begin by looking for small steps.
4. Use creativity in the in-session interventions to help clients understand the ideas. Combine cognition and solution.
5. Assist clients in monitoring their thoughts by writing journal entries between sessions and subsequently reporting cognitions during the next session.

Conclusion

Brief cognitive couple therapy uses a framework for understanding the thought process of couples and attempts to teach couples various techniques for applying the framework to their own case. It combines a solution-focused approach with the cognitive model. The clinician can help the couple further understand how thoughts are played out in behaviors and how a focus on solutions is beneficial. Few people have been taught how to systematically think about their relationship. This suggests that the model for cognitive intervention may be a beneficial part of any attempt to help couples reach solutions.

References

Baucom, D., & Epstein, N. (1990). *Cognitive behavioral marital therapy*. New York: Brunner/Mazel.

de Shazer, S. (1991). *Putting differences to work*. New York: Norton.

Jacobson, N., & Gurman, A. (1995). *Clinical handbook of couple therapy*. New York: Guilford Press.

Lopez, F. G. (1993). Cognitive processes in close relationships: Recent findings and implications for counseling. *Journal of Counseling & Development, 71*, 310–315.

White, M., & Epston, D. (1990). *Narrative means to therapeutic ends*. New York: Norton.

■ ■ ■

9

Modernizing the Genogram: Solutions and Constructions

Patricia Stevens, PhD

The utility of the genogram as an information-gathering tool has been recognized in the family therapy field for many years. Regardless of the theoretical orientation adopted by the counselor for family work, the genogram has proven to be an effective method of gathering large amounts of information about family systems in a small amount of time. In today's managed care world, where therapy is truncated by outside influences, gathering information briefly becomes even more important in order to be effective and economical for third party reimbursements. The graphic representation allowed by the genogram is functional, easy to obtain, and readily available for review.

Using the Genogram

The original purpose of the genogram as posited by Bowen was to examine intergenerational patterns of behavior and emotional processes among at least three generations of the family (McGoldrick & Gerson, 1985). This presentation of patterns allows the counselor to define family membership, ascertain the characteristics of relationships within the family, and discover the mechanisms for

transmission of symptomatic behavior across and between generations (Guerin, 1976). It further encourages clients to make connections concerning the emotional and behavioral problems they are
experiencing and how these problems relate to the "ebb and flow
of the family's emotional processes in their intergenerational context" (Goldenberg & Goldenberg, 1996, p. 181). Constructing the
genogram may be the first time many family members become aware
of the intergenerational patterns of family behavior and emotions.

Information contained in a genogram includes but is not limited to
dates of important events, such as deaths, marriages, divorces, births,
illnesses, and moves; geographical location of family groups; cultural,
ethnic, and religious affiliations; educational and economic levels;
relationships with community and social networks; career information; mental and psychological disorders; and relationships between
and among members. Data presented in this graphic representation
gives the clinician and clients a pictorial view of vast amounts of
family information (Becvar & Becvar, 1996; Nichols & Schwatrz, 1998).

As family therapy has evolved, so has the use of the genogram.
Strategic and structural therapists use the genogram to examine
current family relationships and to gain detailed information of the
here-and-now family dynamics. This information is then used to al-
ter transactions within the family or to design strategies to shift
problematic coalitions or other problem maintaining behaviors in
the family (Becvar & Becvar, 1996; Nichols & Schwatrz, 1998).

Using the Genogram in Solution-Focused Therapy

With the increasing use of the solution-focused therapy model,
the use of the genogram has taken on a different meaning. McGoldrick
and Gerson (1985) were perhaps the first to acknowledge that the
genogram could be used to "reframe behaviors, relationships, and
time connections within families, as well as detoxify and normalize
families' perceptions of themselves" (quoted in Kuehl, 1995, p. 239).

It is also appropriate to address the use of the genogram in the
work of social constructive therapy. Because this theory assumes
that reality is a construction of the observer, using the genogram to
construct a preferred reality can be extremely empowering to the
family. Constructive therapists view the genogram as a means for
assisting the family in understanding and changing the set of assumptions that everyone has about the problem.

Solution-focused therapists believe that clients have the resources
and the ability to solve their own problems but that their lack of

knowledge of alternative behaviors keep them "stuck" in the same unproductive behaviors. It is the counselor's job to assist clients in finding alternative behaviors, many of which are already within clients' repertoire of behavior. One means of facilitating this skill is to find "exceptions" to the problem (de Shazer, 1988) so that clients become aware of alternatives to the repetitive behavior (the problem). Constructive therapies also affirm that clients have the mechanisms to create another reality for themselves and that the counselor's job is to collaborate with clients in constructing a new reality or life story. This may include increasing response options for clients or assisting them in finding "unique outcomes" (White & Epston, 1990). The genogram is a useful tool for either of these endeavors. Because many of the concepts in these two models of counseling are similar, the techniques presented work effectively with either theoretical basis for therapy.

Kuehl (1995) and Huber (1996) both described interventions using a solution-focused genogram. The focus of these interventions is the integration of solution-focused questioning and phrasing with information gathered through use of the genogram. Three examples of the process using these interventions are summarized below.

1. Exceptions and Relative Family Influence

In the same way that solution-focused therapists look for times when the problem does not exist (exceptions), constructive therapists examine the family's ability to prevent the problem from existing all the time or having absolute control over family functioning (relative family influence). The genogram can be particularly helpful with this intervention. Questions are asked regarding the individuals in the family, no matter how distant, who have successfully avoided or "recovered" from the problem. Information is gathered about the ways in which these family members avoided this problem, always focusing on the strengths used by these individuals. In one of his case studies, Kuehl (1995) gave a wonderful example where the counselor tells the client that although "57% of the people in his family have had problems with alcohol, *43% have not* (relative family influence)" (p. 244; emphasis added).

2. Back-to-the-Future Generation Questions

In the "back-to-the-future generation" intervention by Kuehl (1995), the counselor uses a modified version of the miracle question (de Shazer, 1988) to assist clients in recognizing improvement in themselves and making a commitment to future generations in the family. Here are some of the questions one might ask with this intervention: "Given the way it was in your family of origin, and how it is now, describe what you would like it to be different for your children," followed with "So, you are already doing some of those things." This second question leads to collapsing intergenerational time as a means of assisting clients to see that they are already involved in the process of change and solving the problem (Kuehl, 1995; White & Epston, 1990). Other questions that facilitate this intervention: "How are you dealing with this problem differently than your [mother, father] did?" "How are your children benefiting from this change?" and "What is different now than 1 month [1 year; 1 generation] ago?" This intervention implies that the multigenerational transmission process assumed by Bowenians to always be a downward spiral is sometimes a positive shift or improvement from one generation to the next. Bringing this positive change to the client's attention can be extremely empowering.

3. Visual Documentation of Change

The genogram provides a practical and useful method of visually documenting change both across generations and within generations. As the counselor asks positive, change-based questions, this information can be documented on the genogram itself. Kuehl (1995) even suggested using larger and bolder print to record the solutions or exceptions to the problem. Another method of highlighting solutions or improvements would be to use different (brighter) color ink for these positive observations. This provides client with a powerful and visual representation of successes, particularly as the list becomes longer.

Conclusion

The genogram is a widely used information-gathering tool in family therapy. Historically it has been used to record information about clients as well as information about problematic or dysfunctional behavior in the relational dynamics of the family.

Modernizing the genogram enables the counselor to use a well-established and effective mechanism in conjunction with newer therapeutic models. Gathering information that focuses on the positive aspects of the intergenerational family unit (rather than the problems inherent in the system), externalizing the problem, and emphasizing the family's strengths and resiliency creates a genogram that empowers family members. The pictorial story of the family presented by a success–oriented genogram focuses on strengths, not weaknesses; solutions, not problems; and successes, not failures.

References

Becvar, D. S., & Becvar, R. J. (1996). *Family therapy: A systemic integration* (3rd ed.). Boston: Allyn & Bacon

de Shazer, S. (1988). *Clues: Investigating solutions in brief therapy.* New York: Norton.

Goldenberg, I., & Goldenberg, H. (1996). *Family therapy: An overview* (4th Ed.). Pacific Grove, CA: Brooks/Cole.

Guerin, P. J. (1976). *Family therapy: Theory and practice.* New York: Gardner.

Huber, C. H. (1996). Taking an evolutionary perspective: The solution-oriented genogram. *The Family Journal: Counseling and Therapy for Couples and Families, 4,* 152–154.

Kuehl, B. P. (1995). The solution-oriented genogram: A collaborative approach. *Journal of Marital and Family Therapy, 21,* 239–250.

McGoldrick, M., & Gerson, R. (1985). *Genograms in family assessment.* New York: Norton.

Nichols, M. P., & Schwartz, R. C. (1998). *Family therapy: Concepts and methods* (4th ed.). Boston: Allyn & Bacon.

White, M., & Epston, D. (1990). *Narrative means to therapeutic ends.* New York: Norton.

■ ■ ■

10

Using Solution-Focused Techniques With Reconstructed Family Systems

Robert L. Smith, PhD

Family counselors and therapists work with a variety of family systems. According to Glick (1989), approximately 45% of children born in the United States will spend a portion of their lives living with a single parent. Data indicate that 75% of divorced persons remarry within 3 to 4 years and that 60% of them have children, with single-parent and remarriage families comprising nearly 45% of all families (Glick, 1989; Visher & Visher, 1996). When children are involved, reconstructed families are often referred to as *stepfamilies*. Because of the negative connotations associated with the term *stepfamilies*, I use the term *reconstructed family* in this chapter.

The instability of reconstructed families is exacerbated by a lack of positive institutionalized roles for each of the members to play. Problems, or potential problems, are too often emphasized during the early formation of these families. When counselors encounter these family systems for the first time, it is important to consider the context in which the families evolved. Anxiety and turbulence are often present as a result of loss, grief, change, disappointment, fear, mixed loyalties, and other issues associated with divorce, remarriage, and reconstruction. Most families experience this during the early developmental stage of their reconstruction. They have read about the many problems that can occur in newly created families. Too often statistics have been quoted in their presence about the early breakup of such family units. It is not unusual for these families to become problem oriented and overly sensitive to any concern that may surface within their newly constructed family system (Burt & Burt, 1996; Visher & Visher, 1996).

Whereas reconstructed families may easily become problem oriented, counselors should emphasize assets and solutions with these families early in the course of counseling, particularly if the family unit is not in crisis. Using solution-focused techniques may help the family system not only use existing resources, but also reframe the new family in a manner that focuses on and emphasizes positive gains within the system itself. The following solution-focused techniques are useful with reconstructed families; I recommend that they be used in the sequence described in this chapter, possibly over one to three sessions. Many counselors may have used these techniques with individuals, groups, or families. They have been adapted here, however, specifically for use with reconstructed family systems.

Targeting Assets

The technique of targeting assets, aspects of which have been discussed in solution-focused therapy literature (e.g., de Shazer, 1985; O'Hanlon & Weiner-Davis, 1989), specifically focuses on the positive traits and characteristics of each individual in the reconstructed family that help the family as a whole function as a working entity. It helps family members understand what each family member knows about other members and how they can "make the family work." Thus, it allows families to reframe (where appropriate) the entire family unit and view it as a rich environment consisting of capable and talented individuals who may collectively contribute to a successfully operating family system.

Family counselors may begin their work with a family by saying something like the following:

> In newly formed families like yours, there are always pluses and minuses. Maybe some of your friends or relatives have mentioned how hard it is to start over again and successfully create a new family. You may have even heard horror stories about families like yours. Well certainly some of this may be true. However, there is

another side to all of this. When you create a new family, every member brings something into the new family that can help make the family work. This could be a special way you have of listening, talking, or even smiling. It could be a positive attitude that you have or an energy level that seems to pick up everyone else. In any event, my guess is that other family members have seen things in each of you that are positive and will contribute to the success of this family. These characteristics are described as assets that each person possesses. Let's describe these as assets that each person brings to the table (to this family), that will help this family work. To bring these into the open I would like each family member to identify some of the assets or ways of being that other family members bring to the family. Let's begin with . . . [usually one of the children]. Please [to child] turn your chair around [back to others] and listen to the things that other family members see you bringing to the family that are positive and will help make this new family work.

After all family members have spoken, the child turns his or her chair around and repeats what he or she has heard. (The counselor may help summarize.) Each family member takes a turn listening to family members' comments and repeating what he or she has heard. The counselor closes the exercise (or session) by asking family members what they learned about themselves and one another. The counselor challenges family members to identify ways and situations in which they can use what they learned in their everyday family functioning.

This technique, used early in the course of counseling, may help reconstructed families gain greater cohesiveness and trust. It helps to move a family's focus away from blame and fear.

When used with families not in crisis, it has been my experience that this intervention often speeds up the therapeutic process.

Exceptions

Steve de Shazer (1985) and Insoo Kim Berg (DeJong & Berg, 1998) have extensively discussed the idea of searching for and using exceptions in counseling. Using the solution-focused technique Exception Questions, counselors examine past experiences when a problem might reasonably have been expected to occur but somehow did not. Used more broadly, exceptions can be those times when things have gone well with the family unit. When working with reconstructed families that have experienced their share of change and adjustment, counselors can use this technique to help families normalize their circumstances and refocus on what has worked for them thus far. Asking about and examining exceptions may provide families with both hope and support.

Counselors helping a reconstructed family that is not currently experiencing a major crisis might proceed in the following manner:

> With a family like yours, we often hear how difficult and hectic it must have been during this early period of adjustment. There is a tendency to talk about problems or issues between family members. Often these problems do not go away, and in fact they affect everything that is happening within the family system itself. Right now, I would like us to share what has been working so far with this family. Everyone will get a chance to talk, so who wants to begin?

This technique with a reconstructed family often requires an entire session. The counselor plays a supportive and facilitative role during the session. The counselor is curious and asks questions: "How did that happen?" "How did you do that?" "How can you recreate those times?" "When will you be doing things like that again?" This intervention often helps family members understand that they have the resources to be successful, provides hope for family members, and reinforces positive familial interactions.

Family Progress Checklist

Evaluating progress and change in family therapy is essential if treatment is to be successful. Piercy, Sprenkle, and Associates (1986) identified an experiential sculpting exercise used to assess progress. The family sculpting exercise has traditionally involved providing each family member the opportunity to physically sculpt the family structure through the positioning of family members according to the individual's perspective.

As an adaptation of this exercise, the family progress checklist reviews the progress made by the family as related to two variables considered important to healthy family functioning: adaptability and cohesion. Research concerning these two variables states the importance of a balance between family adaptability and cohesion, with extremes representing possible dysfunctional family patterns (Olson, 1986). The progress checklist uses these two variables to assess family progress. According to the Family Environment Scale (Moos & Moos, 1986), *cohesion* is the extent to which family members are concerned and committed to the family and the degree to which family members are helpful and supportive of each other. *Adaptability* is the flexibility within the family to appropriately handle new and difficult situations, whatever they may be. This often means being able to use different approaches and methods in communicating and problem solving.

In using this intervention, the counselor begins by discussing the importance of cohesiveness and adaptability in effective family functioning. The counselor may also wish to discuss research related to these two variables. In some cases the counselor may ask family members to complete the Family Environment Scale and pay special attention to scores on cohesion, expressiveness, conflict, and independence. The counselor defines *cohesiveness* and *adaptability* and may facilitate a brief discussion about the present family's functioning as related to these two variables. When family members understand the variables, the counselor takes 10 steps in an imaginary straight line and places an object at the end of the 10th step. The counselor then asks family members to think of their family again as related to these two variables. The counselor might start with cohesion, writing a definition of the term on a large piece of cardboard paper and placing the cardboard at the end of the 10th step. The counselor then asks each family member to sculpt where he or she perceives family members are as related to this variable. As with any sculpt, questions and discussion evolve around why family members sculpted themselves at a certain place, how comfortable they are, what holds them back (or the family from going further), how they can help the family move forward, and how they might feel when they get there. Family members might also discuss the implications of too much cohesiveness.

The counselor uses the same procedure to assess family adaptability and asks similar focus questions. The counselor facilitates a summary discussion on how these two factors work together and how they relate again to the current family. Following the exercise, the counselor may give homework assignments to help the family move closer to their goals of cohesiveness and adaptability.

This technique is beneficial in at least three ways. First, it introduces the family to variables considered important in healthy family functioning. Second, it affirms the family for progress made and identifies additional steps that individuals, and the family as a whole, can make to develop greater cohesion and adaptability. Third, it provides concrete goals for the family, allowing them to discuss their importance and priority to their family.

Conclusion

In my experience, the techniques discussed in this chapter are helpful for reconstructed family systems. They are useful with a wide range of systems, from large families to couples. I consider them solution-focused in nature because they draw on family members' resources, success, and abilities. Counselors should avoid using these techniques with families in crisis; the techniques are most useful when used with stable family units.

References

Burt, M. S., & Burt, R. B. (1996). *Step families: The step by step model of brief therapy.* New York: Brunner/Mazel.

de Shazer, S. (1985). *Keys to solution in brief therapy.* New York: Norton.

DeJong, P., & Berg, I. K. (1998). *Interviewing for solutions.* Pacific Grove, CA: Brooks/Cole.

Glick, P. C. (1989). Remarried families, stepfamilies, and children: A brief demographic profile. *Family Relations, 28,* 24–27.

Moos, R. H., & Moos, B. S. (1986). *Family environment scale manual* (2nd ed.). Palo Alto, CA: Consulting Psychologists Press.

O'Hanlon, W. H., & Weiner-Davis, M. (1989). *In search of solutions: A new direction for psychotherapy.* New York: Norton.

Olson, D. H. (1986). Circumplex Model VII: Validation studies and FACES III. *Family Process, 25,* 337–351.

Piercy, F. P., Sprenkle, D. H., & Associates. (1986). *Family therapy sourcebook.* New York: Guilford Press.

Visher, E. B., & Visher, J. S. (1996). *Therapy with stepfamilies.* New York: Brunner/Mazel.

■ ■ ■

PART

STRUCTURAL AND STRATEGIC ORIENTED TECHNIQUES

In chapter 11 ("Working With Family Structure Using Wooden Blocks"), William M. Walsh and Michael Furois present the use of blocks as a visible and tactile representation of the client family system structure. They note that blocks are useful in helping discuss past, present, or desired family subsystems and boundaries, rules, roles, and patterns of communication. Although the approach is based on structural and strategic theory, Walsh and Furois state that wooden blocks are useful for addressing family structure issues regardless of one's theoretical orientation.

Robert Sherman, the author of chapter 12 ("Reconstructing Communication: Assuming the Role of Translator"), notes that sender and receiver meaning systems contain biases and assumptions that often result in misperceptions. These misperceptions often lead to (mis)communication that initiates or exacerbates couple and family relationship problems. Sherman explains how counselors, by assuming the role of translator in couple and family counseling, can help clients better understand message (mis)communication and improve their ability to communicate their needs and wants accurately.

In the final chapter of Part II ("Before You Can Conquer the Beast You Must First Make It Beautiful"), Patricia Parr and John Zarski present a technique based on the structural family therapy approach. The technique, which emphasizes family strengths and creativity, encourages the family to enact structural alternatives to scapegoating and conflict. The authors note that this intervention is relatively simple, convenient, and useful with diverse cultural and family configurations.

11

Working With Family Structure Using Wooden Blocks

William M. Walsh, PhD and Michael Furois, PsyD

A holistic perception of family structure originated with Alfred Adler's emphasis on family constellations (Sherman & Dinkmeyer, 1989). Adler's work marked an emergence of theories concerned with the transactions between family members and how that identifies family function or dysfunction. Many family systems theorists have adopted ideas of Adler to develop systemic models that emphasize consistent family transactions within a functional family structure (Sherman & Dinkmeyer, 1989).

The family structure is composed of sets of transactions that form a tightly knit fabric. These transactions determine how family members relate to each other. Structural and strategic theories discuss the quality and regulation of these transactions between subsystems in the family. The two regulating factors in the family system are family subsystems and family boundaries (Minuchin, 1974).

Subsystems are formed on the basis of age or generation, interests, or specific family functions, and their purpose is to carry out various family tasks. There are three basic structural subsystems: adult, parental, and sibling (see Figure 11.1). The adult subsystem is sometimes called the marital or spousal subsystem. It is com-

FIGURE 11.1
Two-Parent, Two Children
Biological Family With Clear Boundaries

H W	adult subsystem (husband and wife)
. . . .	
F M	parental subsystem (father and mother)
. . . .	
B G	sibling subsystem (boy and girl)

posed of the marital dyad or adult partners in the family, and its purpose is to meet the needs of the adults and to teach intimacy and commitment to the children. In a single–parent family, only one adult may be in this subsystem. We view the parental subsystem as one that is composed of the parents, stepparents, or parental surrogates (e.g., grandmother). The major task of this subsystem is responsible child rearing. The sibling subsystem includes all of the children or stepchildren in the family. In this subsystem, the child learns negotiation, cooperation, competition, mutual support, and attachment to friends.

Transactions within and between these subsystems are determined by rules identifying who, and how, a member may participate in each subsystem. These rules are called *boundaries*. They identify the roles, expectations, and consequences the family relies on to maintain homeostasis. Minuchin (1974) identified three levels of boundaries that define subsystem transactions: diffuse, clear, or rigid. Rigid boundaries severely limit communication between and within subsystems and act to provide maximum privacy and minimal interaction. At the other end of the continuum are diffuse boundaries, which are characterized by poorly defined subsystem membership and functions. A diffuse boundary creates little or no privacy, which results in overinvolvement between subsystems. Ideally, the families subsystems demonstrate clear boundaries that promote open communication of roles, expectation, and consequences and create an adequate level of privacy so members can operate freely to fulfill their functions.

Family Mapping

In structural and strategic therapies, the subsystems and boundaries are depicted by family maps. These maps allow the counselor and family to identify areas in family communication patterns for restructuring and thereby set short-term as well as long-term goals. Although less common in today's world, the two-parent biological family may be considered the basic family map. All other maps are variations of this basic format. Figure 11.1 represents the basic map with clear boundaries. Other examples of common family configurations are represented in Figures 11.2, 11.3, and 11.4.

Restructuring a family is based on two principles: (a) A change in any one part of the system affects a change in the entire system, and (b) behavior within the system serves the purpose of maintaining the existing system in the presence of stress; in other words, it promotes homeostasis (Sherman & Fredman, 1986). Challenging transactions in any part of the system and highlighting rigid and

FIGURE 11.2
Single-Parent, Two Children Family
With Diffuse Boundaries

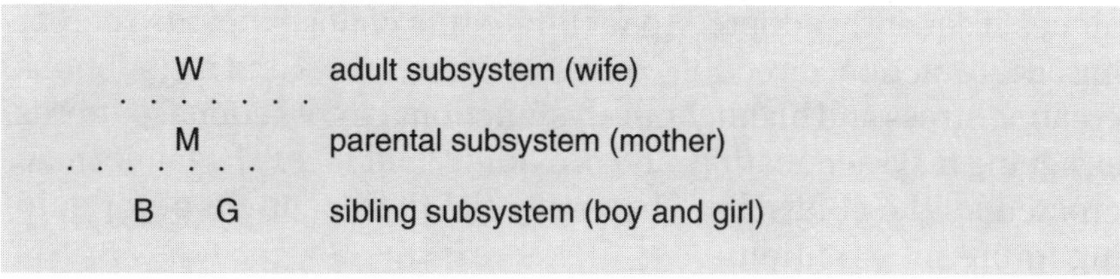

W	adult subsystem (wife)
M	parental subsystem (mother)
B G	sibling subsystem (boy and girl)

FIGURE 11.3
Family Consisting of a Single Mother,
Grandmother (Rose), and Two Children

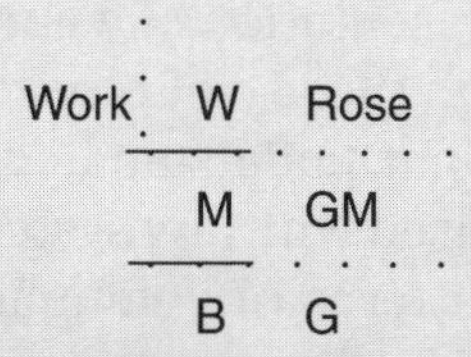

Work W Rose

M GM

B G

Note. There are diffuse boundaries between the mother and her career and rigid boundaries between mother's adult and parent roles and between children. There are diffuse boundaries between the grandmother's adult and parent roles and between the grandmother's parent role and the children.

FIGURE 11.4
Blended Family and Two Maternal Biological Children
With Clear and Rigid Boundaries

exW	H W	exH	adult subsystem (new husband)
	SF M	F	parental subsystem (stepfather, mother)
	B, G, B, G		2 biological children of each adult

Note. In this map, both parents are biological parents of their two children and stepparents of the spouse's two children. The ex-wife has visitation privileges with her children, but a rigid boundary exists with the father of the children and his new wife. The father of the other two children is deceased.

diffuse boundaries prompts the system to seek new solutions. Techniques frequently adopted to facilitate this change include recreating an interaction, directing conversations on rules and negotiations, creating stress and highlighting dysfunctional transactional patterns, assigning tasks, educating, and providing guidance. The family map, created by the counselor, is an essential therapeutic tool for guiding future interventions.

Using Wooden Blocks

We have found that the use of wooden blocks can be used alone or in conjunction with any one of the aforementioned techniques as a visual and tactile representation of a current or future arrangement in the family. Through the use of blocks, families and counselors experience greater insight, understanding, mutuality, and change.

Wooden blocks can be used with any systemic therapy to address family rules, roles, and patterns of communication. Blocks afford tactile representations of healthy systems and transactional patterns. They can be models of interactions occurring in the past, present, or future within and across subgroups in the family. Boundaries can also be demonstrated and highlighted by using common objects to depict the three types of boundaries. Solid objects are good to represent rigid boundaries. Transparent objects (e.g., plastics) work well for clear boundaries. Blank spaces or distance between blocks are good to depict diffuse boundaries. All of these are particularly useful visual aids when trying to explain transactions and rules to families with children.

The blocks initially are presented to the family as a map in the form of a functional system (Figure 11.1). For a family consisting of a mother, father, and two children, two blocks (H) (W) depict the adult subsystem. Beneath them are two blocks (F) (M) to identify the parental subsystem, and on the bottom level are two blocks, each having the first initial of one of the children in the sibling subsystem (Figure 11.5).

With this diagram the counselor can move through each subsystem giving a description of role expectations, behaviors, and tasks that belong to that subsystem:

Counselor: As you can see in this top level, John and Lori, you are the adults in the family. Within this level, interactions exist between both of you as husband and wife such as intimacy, financial activities, and friends. At this level the two of you are concerned with the caring of each other as wife and husband—as adults. Beneath the husband and wife are the behaviors, expectations, and roles of parents. At this level mom and dad are concerned with all parental activities: discipline, cooking meals, cleaning, values, soccer practice, and so on. Here on the bottom of the family map are Jamie and Chris. This level is devoted to age-appropriate behaviors and expectations such as school, friends, chores, sibling interactions, and more.

FIGURE 11.5
General Map of a Family Without Boundaries

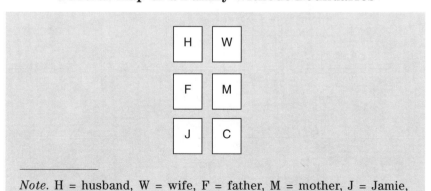

Note. H = husband, W = wife, F = father, M = mother, J = Jamie, C = Chris.

From this point the explanation–education can turn to bound-aries. The counselor can enhance the family map by adding bound-aries to the block configuration and capture the children's interest by using different candies to demonstrate boundaries (perhaps lico-rice to represent rigid boundaries, M&Ms to demonstrate diffuse boundaries, and a row of Tootsie Rolls to depict a clear boundary). It can be particularly powerful to model the family as it exists in the room (see Figure 11.4).

Counselor: John, you just said that you have Jamie (the youngest child) sleeping with you and Lori in bed at night. I also remem-ber, Lori, you stated that one of your goals for therapy was to improve the intimacy in your marriage. Is it possible that this arrangement creates a lack of privacy between your adult and parental subsystems? This is what is referred to as a diffuse boundary, a system of rules in your family that does not allow adequate privacy between you as adults and as parents. [pause and discuss with the family]

Counselor: This may also compromise your expectation that Jamie should become less "clingy" to you both. The diffuse boundary does not allow Jamie to develop the independence and self-sufficiency she needs to stop the clinging behavior (Figure 11.6)

Demonstration with blocks of past transactions, (e.g., re-enact-ment) is another way to bring experiential exercises into the ses-sion. Family members can see how the transaction was carried out,

FIGURE 11.6
General Map of a Family With Diffuse Boundaries

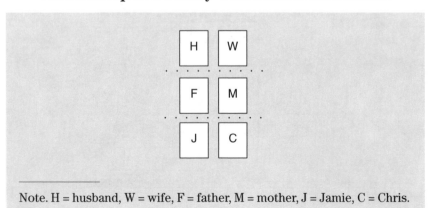

Note. H = husband, W = wife, F = father, M = mother, J = Jamie, C = Chris.

share with the family how that event affected them, and demonstrate other transactional possibilities with the blocks.

Counselor: John, you mentioned that last week the family went to purchase a new family car. You also said that you had disagreed with Lori on her choice of cars but didn't say anything because Chris and Lori both thought it to be the best option. This seems to be an example when there was too little communication, a rigid boundary, at the adult level and perhaps Chris was pulled up into the adult subsystem. [At this point, the counselor pulls Chris's block into the adult system; see Figure 11.7.]

This technique may have the greatest impact when it is used to demonstrate an interaction as it is happening. We have found that it is difficult to increase the awareness of clients "in the moment" regarding a transaction that has just occurred. Perhaps the emotional charge of the session interferes with their comprehension. Yet, when blocks are used, understanding seems to increase as the focus is not so much on the clients but on their interaction as depicted by the blocks.

Counselor: Lori, let me stop you for a minute. Just now it seemed that you and John were having a hard time agreeing on the appropriate way to confront Chris's teacher. I noticed then that you brought Chris in to make the final decision on how this

FIGURE 11.7
Family Map Depicting Invasion
of Child Into the Adult Subsystem

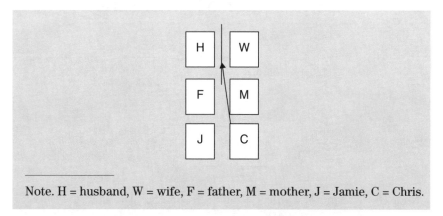

Note. H = husband, W = wife, F = father, M = mother, J = Jamie, C = Chris.

should be done. This seems to be an instance of Chris being pulled into the Parental Subsystem. [At this time the counselor is moving Chris's block into the parental level; see Figure 11.8.] Chris, what was it like for you to make that decision after hearing both of your parents wishes?

As a system becomes more complicated, the need to concretely map the family structure becomes greater. As stepfamilies become the norm rather than the exception, blocks can be particularly useful in showing a complicated series of family transactions. Let us consider working with a divorced man with two children coming into the family of a woman with two children (e.g., Figure 11.3). The idiosyncratic nature of families regarding differences in rules, roles, expectations, and consequences creates conflict as the two systems attempt to blend. Blocks in this situation allow the blended family to move each distinct system to separate the expectations of one system from the new, blended system.

Counselor: In your previous marriage, Craig, you had not allowed the children to eat in the living room. The rule was that everyone was to eat at the same time around the family table if they were to eat that night, correct? This is the expectation of this system. (See Figure 11.9) Sherry has said that their schedules prevented them from eating together. Sherry, you stated that everyone was always doing their own thing and eating on their

FIGURE 11.8
Intrusion of Child Into the Parental Subsystem With Diffuse Boundaries

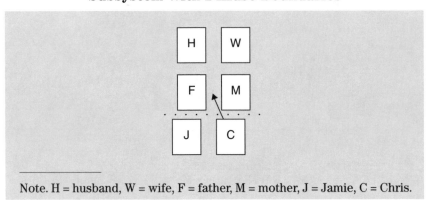

Note. H = husband, W = wife, F = father, M = mother, J = Jamie, C = Chris.

own when they got a chance. This was the expectation of this system. (See Figure 11.9) You are in a process of blending the two and finding mutual expectations when both of you have such different ideas of what is best. How can we find a compromise in this situation? (See Figure 11.9, Step 2.)

It can be particularly useful to show individuals as they come into or out of the system and the effect this has on the system (e.g., leaving for the weekend with the other parent).

When the number of elements in the family system increases, the utility of blocks follows. Blocks can be used to represent activities, organizations, behaviors, and so on. Recently we worked

FIGURE 11.9
Change From Two Biological Families
to One Blended Family

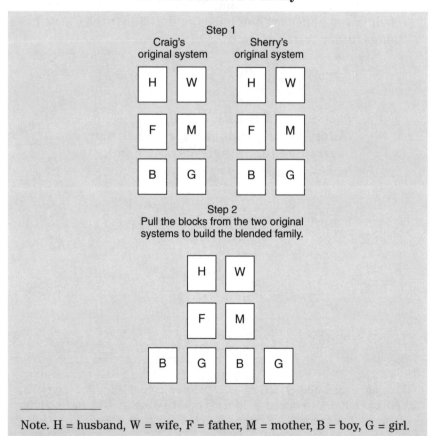

Note. H = husband, W = wife, F = father, M = mother, B = boy, G = girl.

with a family where numerous factors—single parent, grandmother, a career, and alcoholism—all played a part in the structural dysfunction of this family. In sessions with this family, each element of the family's system was represented by a block in an attempt to highlight the effect of each part of the system on the others. We had the usual blocks of (W) (M) (B) (G), to which we added the blocks T (grandmother's first name), C (career), and A (alcoholism). (See Figure 11.10.) In the following example the counselor picks up the blocks and moves them as they are describing the situation.

Counselor: Lois, you had asked your mother to come live with you because you are out of town frequently, is that true? Yet, when you described last week's events while you were away on business, it seems that you communicated to Carry (female and the oldest child) information that might be most appropriate for a parent. For example, what to get at the grocery store, when Justin should go to bed, and so on. Do your concerns with Thelma's alcohol use enter into your decision to tell Carry these things rather than Thelma?

FIGURE 11.10
Addition of Grandmother and Other
Variables to a Single-Parent Family

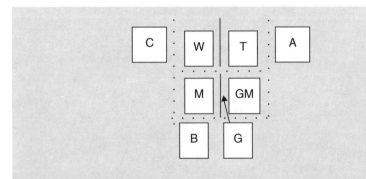

Note. The blocks are used to help the family identify structural problems such as the involvement of Mom's career on her adult and parenting (M) roles. Grandmother's (GM) alcoholism was highlighted; so too was its effect on the system with a diffuse boundary, mistrust by the mother, and the pulling up of the daughter into the parental role.

Conclusion

Using wooden blocks is a useful means to help families better understand existing or desired family structures. When the blocks are introduced, the only element limiting their use is the counselor's imagination. We have observed families understanding the technique very quickly and taking it on themselves to move the blocks to demonstrate a transaction. In our training of family counselors, we have used blocks to re-enact scenes from a session to increase the counselor's understanding of the family map and how to work with it in session. It has become such a widely used technique in our training program that we joke about making it required material along with the text.

References

Minuchin, S. (1974). *Families and family therapy*. Cambridge, MA: Harvard University Press.

Sherman, R., & Dinkmeyer, D. (1989). *Systems of family therapy: An Adlerian integration*. New York: Brunner/Mazel.

Sherman, R., & Fredman, N. (1986). *Handbook of structured techniques in marriage and family therapy*. New York: Brunner/Mazel.

■ ■ ■

12

Reconstructing Communication: Assuming the Role of Translator

Robert Sherman, EdD

When communication is stuck in antiquated, toxic, or confusing patterns, the counselor may find it useful to step into the role of translator. As translator, the counselor is able to constructively clarify, reframe, refocus, and shift the meanings of the communication and interpret underlying feelings and needs. By changing the tone and constructively rephrasing the content, the counselor may be able to move communication forward in line with the agreed upon goals of counseling.

Regardless of their theoretical orientations, counselors consistently seek to clarify and better understand the meaning of client communications, as well as to generate perceptual alternatives, by asking questions, making educated guesses, reframing ideas, communicating emotion, and checking out their perceptions with clients. Communication takes place at many levels, and metacommunications—such as body language, tone of voice, inflection, built-in expectations, and assumptive values, history, custom, tradition, and context—may be more important than the actual words used. Counselors seek to understand the metacommunication and encourage client awareness of it. In the role of translator, the counselor can integrate these processes into a single intervention.

Clients frequently communicate by complaining, attacking, withdrawing, withholding, lying, constructing unending and confusing explanations, and using various defense mechanisms. They are typically stuck in a pattern of communication and a personal framework of meanings that also includes projections about what other family members are thinking, feeling, and doing.

They therefore hear others in that context and may misperceive the intentions of communicators. The translator can identify such misperceptions and reconstruct the communications to convey the clients' true intentions.

Every person has a unique style and language of communication (Sherman, Oresky, & Rountree, 1991; Sherman, Shumsky, & Rountree, 1994). People express love, anger, fear, joy, appreciation, caring, and most other emotions in their own unique way and with different degrees of intensity. If one partner does not communicate love and appreciation in the other partner's favored form, the expressions may have minimal or even the opposite effect. For example, if a husband's way of loving is to do things for his wife but his wife is struggling to achieve a sense of independence, then she may experience his way of loving as stifling. She may resist or criticize her husband, and he may feel rejected and unappreciated.

The counselor translator who is not stuck in problematic patterns of communication may hear and perceive more accurately. The perceptions can be presented as translations to be evaluated for accuracy by the person communicating. In acting as a translator, the counselor can also model effective modes of communication for the couple or family. In effect, the translations become alternative constructions of reality.

When the counselor thinks that assuming the role of translator may be a useful intervention, he or she asks, "Would it be all right if I translate for you what I think you are saying to [the other person], and will you tell us if I'm representing you correctly?" If the client agrees, the counselor proceeds. The counselor can similarly translate for the others to restructure the entire pattern of communication.

Dealing With Hostility: Softening the Message

Marilyn: You didn't even call to find out how I was yesterday when I was feeling so sick.

James: You never remember to pick up my shirts from the cleaners.

Counselor: May I translate for you both, and you will tell me if I'm correct. [They agree.] Are you saying, Marilyn, that James is really important to you and you really need him, especially when you are feeling vulnerable like when you're sick, but at other times too?

Marilyn: Yes. He's the one I want to be there for me. And I should be important enough to him.

Counselor: James, you're really important to me, and I need to know that I'm important to you too.

Counselor: Do you understand that James?

James: Yes.

Counselor: Is it okay that she thinks you're important and wants to be important to you, too?

James: Sure. She is important to me.

Counselor: And is it okay for you to pay more attention to her, especially when she is vulnerable about something, but also in general?

James: Yes, but whatever I do is not enough. She always has some complaint or objection.

Counselor: Is this what you are saying now and what you were trying to say before, James? "Marilyn, when you criticize me or don't appreciate the things I do, I get hurt and then I get mad, so I criticize you or stay away from you. And because it hurts so much, it is very hard for me to admit when you are right or partly right in your criticism. It makes me feel like a bad person."

James: I guess so.

Counselor: Do you mean yes? If any part of it is wrong, please correct it now.

James: It's right.

Counselor: Do you understand, Marilyn, that it hurts him when he is criticized?

Marilyn: Yes, but how can I let him know what I want?

Counselor: That's a good question. Are you ready to discover how you can be less critical, Marilyn, and are you ready to discover how you can be more attentive, James, so that you can both get more of what you want? You may also want to learn why attention is so important to you, Marilyn, and why you are so sensitive to criticism, James. Are you ready for that?

Both: Yes.

In this intervention, the focus of attention was shifted from complaining and attacking to mutual needs and mutual validation of those needs.

Dealing With Passivity: Hardening the Message

Counselor: Peter has been telling you very clearly what things he expects of you and complains angrily that you don't deliver. How is that for you?

Ellen: Well, he's right, but I can't seem to get to all those things and do them the way he wants them done.

Counselor: May I try to translate for you what you are telling Peter, and will you tell me if I'm correct?

Ellen: Sure.

Counselor: "Peter, the truth is that I resent that you're always telling me what to do as though you are my boss or my father, and when you do that then I really don't want to do anything. I can be responsible, but I need to do things according to my schedule." Is that correct?

Ellen: Yes, he treats me like a child.

Counselor: Are you willing to tell Peter to get off your back? If so, tell him now.

Ellen: Get off my back, and I will take care of most of those things.

Peter: Yes, but you don't do them, and I get very upset. These things have to get done. What I tell you is common sense, and I don't understand why you can't see that.

Counselor: Are you saying to Ellen, "I need to be in charge or in control or else I get very anxious and I can't deal with that anxiety. I need for you to do it my way to make me feel better."?

The translations continue until it is understood that Peter is playing the role of Inspector General–Boss to control his anxieties, and Ellen is playing the rebellious and withholding child to protect her selfhood from domination and belittlement. Notice that Ellen is helped to assert herself, and Peter's vulnerability is made known so that the dispute can be properly framed in a more balanced way, and they can move onto better understandings and solutions.

Dealing With Confusion: Clarifying the Messages

For the person who goes on endlessly trying to make a point, the counselor may briefly summarize the point the client is attempting to make. The counselor can then teach the person to say what is important in a few sentences and to put a period at the end of the sentence. They can work on how to stop even if a strong feeling of anxiety pushes the person to continue in order to make sure he or she is understood. Translating a "yes, but" or double-bind message, as in the following example, can be fun.

Alex: Yes, I want to make plans for our vacation, but you usually plan things that I don't agree with, and I wish you would be more considerate of me.

Counselor: Sue, Alex is saying to you that although he likes the fact that you are taking the initiative in planning your vacation together, he doesn't trust that you will plan for things that are considerate of his fears and phobias even though he really would love to do some of those things himself. So he has to reject your ideas. He doesn't really mean to blame you for his fears, but he is frustrated and angry about the limitations he imposes on himself. Is that correct, Alex?

Every communication contains built-in assumptions. If the counselor's translation is accepted, then Alex accepts responsibility for the consequences of his phobia instead of setting his wife up for criticism and blame.

Conclusion

Counselor translations may be used as a cognitive approach to help clients better understand their beliefs, feelings, and behaviors. They can help to clarify communication or make the communication more effective. They can shift the focus to highlight or emphasize different aspects of the communication, situation, or relationship. They can modify the mood by creating a shift from the negative to the positive. They can be used to reduce toxicity; clarify messages; get to the bottom of feelings, beliefs, and expectations; and reconcile differences in individual languages and styles of expression. They can help clients to change their framework of meanings and to reconstruct their perceptions of reality.

Note: Portions of this chapter are taken from "The Therapist as Translator: Reconstructing Communication," by R. Sherman, 1996, *The Family Journal*, 4, 69–71. Copyright 1996 by the American Counseling Association. Adapted by permission.

References

Sherman, R., Oresky, P., & Rountree, Y. (1991). *Solving problems in couples and family therapy: Techniques and tactics.* New York: Brunner/Mazel.

Sherman, R., Shumsky, A., & Rountree, Y. (1994). *Enlarging the therapeutic circle: The therapist's guide to collaborative therapy with families and schools.* New York: Brunner/Mazel.

■ ■ ■

13

Before You Can Conquer the Beast You Must First Make It Beautiful

Patricia Parr, PhD and John Zarski, PhD

A basic tenet of structural family therapy is that all functioning is the product of the structure of the system from which it springs, so that a change in structure produces change in functioning. Thus, structural interventions with families dealing with issues of adolescence must be able to disrupt or supercede the existing structure and offer family members alternative ways to carry out their function. According to Fishman (1988),

> The existence of a disturbed adolescent in a family serves as the silent canary does in a mine—it is a tipoff that there are problems in the system. In addition to being strongly affected by the family context, adolescents in turn affect the context of which they are a part. The very presence of a troubled adolescent in the family creates pressures that require the therapist to pay attention to other family members. (p. 5)

When working with families, our focus is on modifying or altering common dysfunctional structures, including problems with boundaries, dysfunctional alignments, and power issues. In evaluating the family, the counselor must develop a clear understanding of the problem. To this end, the counselor (a) searches for what family functions are being blocked by the symptom and (b) seeks to discover how the problem is maintained in the system. To accomplish these objectives, the counselor attends to the relationship structures among family members and others in the social context of the problem. There is no better way to understand these sustaining structures than by seeing and experiencing them in action through the use of enactments. As families "enact" or spontaneously act out new ways of relating, the counselor can investigate the variety and flexibility of the structures and intervene directly in the transactions of the family to bring about change. The family counselor assumes an active, involved role. Like the director of a play, he or she observes and encourages intrafamilial transactions in order to stimulate or provoke change.

The technique may be introduced to the family in the following manner:

> Over the last several weeks I've been noticing something very interesting about the way you talk to each other; in fact, it reminds me of the fairy tale "Goldilocks and the Three Bears," which tells you something about my age. Let me explain. It seems to me that Mary (problem adolescent) is trying very hard to be a part of this family but each time she tries to fit in the chair, it is either too big or too small and everyone ends up annoyed or angry and nobody has the chance to talk about building or finding a chair that is the right fit for her.

Using this opening, the counselor invites the family to consider alternatives to scapegoating and conflict. When it becomes apparent that Mary's development has stagnated and that she is behaving in inappropriate ways, the counselor can invite the family to play and be creative. This may facilitate boundary change, and a healing process can begin.

At this point, the counselor might describe a personal family-of-origin experience in which family members made gifts for one another on holidays and birthdays. The counselor suggests that perhaps the family in counseling might enjoy a break in routine to do something different and fun. The counselor may then suggest a homework assignment of using clay dough to create their individual versions of Mary, the "ideal adolescent." The counselor suggests that Mary focus on her soccer practice during the following week while other members of the family are provided clay dough for their project.

At the following session, each family member is asked to provide Mary with her gift, along with a description of positive traits and qualities. In closing, Mary is offered the possibility that she no longer needs to try out anyone else's chair—she is allowed to have her own unique way of fitting in with the family.

This technique has been useful with many different family configurations, including intact, single-parent, and even sibling subsystems. It is simple to use and is relatively convenient; the clay dough may be purchased at discount stores. The technique emphasizes family strengths and creativity and can be varied to better match the family's cultural, ethic, or racial background.

Note. The title of this chapter is a Chinese proverb.

Reference

Fishman, H. C. (1988). *Treating troubled adolescents: A family therapy approach.* New York: Basic Books.

■ ■ ■

PLAY THERAPY AND PARENT–CHILD TECHNIQUES

According to Daniel S. Sweeney, the author of chapter 14 ("Sandplay With Couples"), sandplay is "a play therapy modality, which provides clients the opportunity to access and confront issues through the process and projection onto miniature objects in a sandtray." He states that sandplay originated from Jungian theory but has evolved to a more eclectic intervention because counselors espousing various theoretical perspectives find it useful. Sweeney's chapter includes a brief overview describing the purpose of and materials needed for sandplay and explains how counselors can use this creative approach to help couples process critical issues.

In chapter 15 ("Create-a-Game"), Karin B. Jordan discusses her creative use of game-playing strategy in couple and family counseling. The author notes that Create-a-Game is especially useful when counseling families with school-age children. This structured, highly interactive technique helps to engage both children and adults and is useful in working with a range of social and developmental needs.

S. Allen Wilcoxon, the author of chapter 16 ("Permission to Speak Freely: Consent and Intervention With the Noncustodial Parent and Children"), notes that, although helping families experiencing divorce has been an emphasis in the professional counseling literature, the primary focus has been on working with the custodial parent and children, as well as stepparents and stepchildren. In this chapter, Wilcoxon provides suggestions on issues of consent and intervention for counselors working with the unique and neglected configuration of noncustodial parent and children in counseling.

Chapter 17 ("The School-Based Family Counseling Classroom Checklist Procedure"), by Michael J. Carter and William P. Evans, presents an intervention based on a school-based family counseling (SBFC) process model for addressing classroom difficulties. The authors explain how the SBFC classroom checklist procedure is used to increase parent and child awareness of classroom behavior, provide feedback regarding the effectiveness of other classroom-focused interventions, and improve the relationship between parents and child.

Michael S. Nystul, in chapter 18 ("Emotional Balancing: A Parenting Technique to Enhance Parent–Child Relationships"), notes that parent education programs typically focus on helping parents develop appropriate behaviors and attitudes. However, the concept of "parental emotions" appears to be a neglected dimension in the parenting literature. Nystul describes a parental emotions model and then presents an emotional balancing procedure that assists parents in making effective emotional connections with their children.

Asking family members to discuss their daily routines is a useful means of assessing the relationships between parents and children and between siblings. The final chapter, by Frances Y. Mullis ("How Was Your Day? Using Questions About the Family's Daily Routine"), presents useful questions for eliciting daily routine information and discusses how this information can provide valuable insight into current family functioning and direction for improvement of the same.

■ ■ ■

14

Sandplay With Couples

Daniel S. Sweeney, PhD

Couple counseling and therapy offer multiple challenges for the marriage and family counselor. It is not unusual to find one or both partners reluctant to actively participate in the therapeutic process. The presenting issues are frequently complex and entrenched, because most couples delay seeking treatment until a crisis develops. By then, patterns of communication and metacommunication are often difficult to assess. A creative and projective intervention such as sandplay provides a safe and expressive avenue for the couple in crisis to present and process critical issues in therapy.

Sandplay offers clients the opportunity to process painful issues without having to directly verbalize them. When partners in a couple relationship are unwilling or unable to verbally express themselves in their daily relationship and during the counseling process, a nonverbal means of expression is a welcome tool in therapy. Sandplay is a play therapy modality that provides clients the opportunity to access and confront issues through the process and projection onto miniature objects in a sand tray.

Sandplay allows the couple to create "world" pictures in the sand tray, giving the counselor and each partner an opportunity to view relationship and communication dynamics. What a partner does or does not contribute to the process is a reflection of the investment that he or she has in the relationship. The frequent "dance" that individuals and couples do to avoid core issues emerges, creating an opportunity for a new waltz to begin. Triangles and the related emotional processes can be identified and resolved.

The interactional sequence described by Guerin, Fay, Burden, and Kautto (1987) becomes particularly clear in the sandplay process. Conflictual marriages are described as typically involving a pursuit and distancing pattern; this pattern may be evident to the couple or counselor at some level, and it is further identified in the sand tray. Identification of this reciprocal pattern is crucial to the resolution of couple conflict, so that new relationship and communication skills can be taught. Sandplay, therefore, can be used as both an evaluatory and training tool in treatment.

Some couples are willing and able to process their issues on a verbal level, and they should not be forced into using sandplay in the counseling office. However, even these couples may be consciously or unconsciously denying an important concern that may emerge in the sandplay process.

Sandplay is both a specific theoretical and technical orientation to treatment. The counselor who uses sandplay in practice should receive adequate training and supervised experience. Simply put, sandplay with couples requires expertise with both sandplay and couples therapy. This short chapter is intended both to educate and to whet the appetite of readers interested in using sandplay in couple or family therapy.

What Is Sandplay?

Although originally developed as a therapeutic intervention for children, sandplay can be used with clients of all ages. Its use with couples, families, and groups has been increasing, although the majority of the sandplay literature seems to be focused on work with individual clients.

It would be helpful to take a brief look at the history of sandplay. Dr. Margaret Lowenfeld (1979) first developed the therapeutic use of the sand tray and miniatures in London in the 1920s. She had read H. G. Wells's (1911) book *Floor Games*, in which Wells talked about his playing with miniature toys on the floor with his two sons, and she was determined to adopt the concept therapeutically. Lowenfeld used a sand tray and miniatures with children, asking them to create "world pictures." This technique was later called the *Lowenfeld world technique.* Dora Kalff (1980), a Swiss Jungian analyst, adopted Lowenfeld's technique and developed a variation called *sandplay*. Although the term *sandplay* has historically been a Jungian term, the increased use of the sand tray as a medium by counselors espousing various theoretical orientations has led to use of the term in a more generic sense.

In sandplay, the client (whether child or adult) "has the opportunity to resolve the traumas through externalizing the fantasy and by developing a sense of relationship and control over inner impulses through play" (Allan, 1988, p. 154). Like play therapy and other expressive therapies, sandplay allows clients to "talk" about their issues without having to verbalize. Clients of any age can approach and process emotional issues within the safety of the modality, managing their issues through the placement and manipulation of the sandplay miniatures. For the couple or partner who is reluctant to verbalize issues of conflict, the therapeutic distance (and corresponding safety) that sandplay provides makes the processing of delicate issues much easier.

Sandplay meets a number of emotional needs for couples. Lois Carey (1990) suggested several therapeutic rationales for the use of sandplay, which essentially summarize its benefits. First, sand is tactile and provides a total kinesthetic experience for the couple. Sometimes relatively nonverbal clients start running their fingers through the sand in the tray and simply begin to talk, as though the sensation of the sand loosens their tongue. Although this is neither the intent nor the goal, it may be a therapeutic byproduct. Second, limits are naturally set by the size of the sand tray, which ultimately leads partners to develop their own limit-setting skills. Whereas boundaries are a primary issue in the process of couple therapy, it would seem important that therapeutic interventions assist both partners to develop common and individual boundaries and to cultivate an internal locus of control. An additional factor is that sandplay allows the couple to have total control over the construction and action of the tray and thus to have an increased sense of power. In most cases of couple therapy, one or both partners feel disempowered and out of control. Thus, providing a treatment modality that does not directly challenge a likely power-imbalanced system is often helpful.

Furthermore, sandplay can encourage verbalization in cases where clients have poor verbal skills and provide a safe place for those clients who use verbalization as a defense. Although verbalization is not always a goal of the sandplay intervention, it can give words to previously unspoken emotional issues. Clients who use verbalization as a defense and are verbally sophisticated do not necessarily know how to express deep emotional needs. Sandplay may cut through these defenses. Another benefit of using sandplay is that transference issues can be handled by the sand tray, with miniatures (rather than the counselor) becoming the transference vessel. Although transference is a natural, expected, and often beneficial process in therapy, it is usually best to keep the focus on the couple. Negative transference issues can be decreased or neutralized with the projective approach of sandplay. A final benefit of sandplay is that deeper issues may be accessed more quickly than with other treatment modalities; the sand provides a safe venue in which to disclose and process, and the sand and miniatures assist in making concrete that which is abstract.

The basic equipment necessary for sandplay may be very rudimentary or quite elaborate and detailed. It is not necessary to invest a great deal of office space or thousands of dollars in building a collection of sandplay miniatures, as many do. The basics include two sand trays and a selection of miniatures.

The sand trays themselves are normally 20 inches × 30 inches × 3 inches, painted blue on the inside, to simulate sky and water, and are half filled with fine sand. It is best not to use playground sand, which often has small pebbles in it, or sand that is too fine, because its powdery quality may be harmful for the allergy-prone counselor. The size of the trays is important; it should be small enough to provide boundaries and limits for the client and to enable the contents of the trays to be viewed in a single glance. Two trays are desirable, and they should be waterproof, so that one can be used for wet sand and the other for dry sand. If only one tray is available, and clients want to use water in it, the counselor is stuck with wet sand for all remaining clients until the sand can be replaced. The trays should be set on a stable surface, preferably on a table that is about average desk height, and has some room around the base of the tray. It is useful to have trays on a mobile cart that can be moved from one corner of the therapy room to the middle as needed.

A selection of miniatures is then made available for use in the sand. The miniatures should be about 2–3 inches in height. These should be selected for the sandplay process—not collected. Although it is not necessary to have thousands of miniatures, it is helpful to have a wide assortment of toys and objects. Some basic categories include the following:

- buildings (houses, castles, factories, schools, churches, stores)
- people (various racial and ethnic groups, military, cowboys, sports figures, fantasy, mythological, various occupations)
- vehicles (cars, trucks, planes, boats, emergency vehicles, farm equipment, military vehicles)

- animals (domestic, farm, zoo, wild, marine, prehistoric)
- vegetation (trees, shrubs, plants)
- deities (crosses, madonnas, menorahs, nativity sets)
- structures (fences, bridges, gates, highway signs)
- natural objects (rocks, shells, driftwood, feathers)
- miscellaneous (jewelry, wishing wells, treasure chests)

It is important to be sensitive to issues of diversity in the selections of miniatures. It is especially important to have miniature people (of both genders) reflecting a variety of ethnocultural groups. For example, in a predominately Asian community one should never provide sandplay with a miniature collection containing only Caucasian figures. Similarly, it is helpful to be sensitive to other issues, such as geography; for example, it makes sense to have miniature cacti when working in a desert community and pine trees when working in the forest town.

Miniatures should be grouped by category and preferably displayed on open shelves. Clients are simply less likely to rummage through drawers or bins than they are to select objects from a shelf. The categorization is important, because the emotionally fragile client is less likely to select a miniature kitten if it is set right next to a fire–breathing dragon, and the impatient and reticent client is often unwilling to search at all. For the busy counseling office, a bookcase on the side of the therapy room with some type of cover (so that it is not a distraction when not being used) works well.

A modest yet broad collection of miniatures is more than adequate. Building up a collection of miniatures can be quite expensive, so the beginning sandplay therapist should check out garage sales and thrift stores. It is often cheaper to buy a bride and groom from a wedding cake shop, or a bridge from a discount aquarium store, then it is to order miniatures from a sand tray miniature catalog. The trays themselves can also be expensive but are relatively easy to make. I made mine from pine wood that I painted and waterproofed. In a pinch it is easy to use a plastic sweater box with a blue cover, which can be placed under the clear plastic to simulate the blue bottom of the tray.

Sandplay With Couples

The process of the sandplay varies depending on the theoretical orientation and style of the counselor. The level of the counselor's involvement in the sandplay process may range from very little direct involvement and comment (a more Jungian approach) to being very active and making several comments and asking questions (a more Gestalt approach). In this section I describe my approach to using sand trays and miniatures with couples.

Most often, I simply ask the couple to create a tray together. I briefly explain the modality and process and request that the couple give informed consent. Couple conflicts undoubtedly involve communication challenges, so I explain to the couple that because I really do not know them well, I would like to use a communication tool that allows them to express their concerns in nonverbal ways. In my experience, some clients enthusiastically endorse the modality and want to dive in, and others see it as frivolous or child's play. I am not particularly interested in converting the doubters, but I find that most couples are willing to participate after they receive adequate explanation.

The creation of a tray together allows me to observe the partners as they live and relate. I introduce the sand tray and miniatures to couples by suggesting that they look over the miniatures and then create a "picture" or "world" in the sand. My instructions are generally no more specific than this, with the exception of providing a prompt for those couples who are having a difficult time beginning the tray. An example of this prompt may be simply to ask them to construct a scene reflecting the past weekend or holiday.

As the couple begins to select the miniatures and place them in the sand, my own involvement in and reflection on the process varies, depending on my sense of the couple's relationship. At times I make frequent reflective comments and engage in dialogue with the couple as they work, using the couple and the general tenor of the session as my guide. Sometimes I say very little, primarily with the intent to honor and reverence the construction of the tray (which is essentially the uncovering of intrapsychic and interpersonal issues), a key element in the Jungian approach. The majority of the interaction occurs at the completion of the tray, when I begin to ask questions.

As the couple constructs the tray, the counselor should consider the following questions; the answers to these questions may provide the insight into the couple's relational dynamics:

1. Who initiates the construction of the sand tray world? Who ends the process?
2. What objects are considered, selected, and rejected? By whom? Are one partner's suggestions or sections rejected by the other partner?

3. Does the couple work together to construct the tray? Are there two separate worlds created in the one tray?
4. Were friendly or hostile messages sent by either partner? Did either one send a "you do your thing and I'll do mine" kind of message?
5. Who contributed the most? What is the percentage of space used by either partner?
6. Does the couple talk to each other during the process? Do they decide on a theme? If so, do both follow the theme?
7. Is the process structured or chaotic?

The answers to these questions may provide essential information about the couple's relationship. The degree of participation, reactivity, compartmentalization, territorialism, reactivity, compliance, and rejection (the list may go on) observed in the construction of the tray should be a direct reflection of the couple's typical interactions.

After they construct the tray, I normally begin by asking them what the title of the world is. It is a rare occurrence that a couple (at least one of the partners) does not come up with a title. I then ask them to tell a story about the tray. In individual sandplay, I ask the client to tell me about the scene, to take me into his or her world. With couples, I usually ask them to talk with each other about the tray, to take each other into the world of the tray. This may be a challenge for the couple with communication problems, and the counselor may have to assist in this process. I next want the couple to tell me about the tray, to take me into their world. It is important to give both partners equal opportunity to share.

This process includes a great deal of material coming out through the story, and I often elicit further information by asking questions: What about this figure here? What is she doing? It looks like these two are saying something to each other—what could they be talking about? Are you (either partner) in this picture? Is there anyone else you know in here? What's going to happen next (if it is an active scene)? What (not who) has the most power here? A number of other questions may come up within the process, but I try to keep them simple and open-ended and to avoid questions that are intrusive or that jump to a conclusion.

I am also interested in the couple processing the experience with me. What was it like for both of them?

I sometimes ask couples to each create a tray side by side. I do this when I have a sense that one or both of the partners is unwilling or unable to adequately express themselves in a joint tray. The joint tray may be too threatening to do; one or both may withdraw in the creation of a joint tray but be able to more fully express and create on an individual basis. When couples create individual trays, I normally discourage them from talking during the creation of the worlds. After they complete the trays, I ask each partner whether he or she is willing to share about the tray, and I encourage or coach the other partner in active listening. Interruptions are not allowed, and equal time is given to talk, even if the time is not used.

I ask many of the same types of questions listed above about each tray, and I also like to encourage the couple to talk with each other about each other's tray (similarities, differences, and so on). This may be a first time for a couple to talk about expectations and goals for their relationship, which often are manifested in the two trays.

Allan (1988) discussed common stages in the sandplay process with children, which I have found to be helpful in assessing the progress of sandplay with couples. The first stage is chaos, in which the couple may "dump" miniatures into the sand, often without any apparent deliberate selection. The chaos evident in the sand is reflective of the chaos and emotional turmoil in the couple's life. Most marriage and family counselors are familiar with the dumping of issues that couples do in the therapy room. The next stage described is struggle, in which there may be overt or covert conflict, even "battle" scenes. At the beginning of the creation of these scenes, often the two (or more) sides in the fight annihilate each other. In other words, the world depicts a no-win situation. Although the scene may reflect one side winning (e.g., a dominant partner over an unassertive, compliant partner), it really is not a win–lose situation, it is a lose–lose situation. I have often found in the early stages of sandplay, with children and adults, that no one survives these battles or accidents. With positive progress, and the process of building relationship and communication, the sandplay therapy moves to the third stage, which Allan describes as *resolution*, where life seems to be "getting back to normal." There is more order and balance in the tray, miniatures are deliberately selected and carefully placed, and the couple sees themselves in the trays, often in helpful and egalitarian roles. This is usually a sign that therapy can be brought to an end.

It is important to talk about the issue of interpretation in the process of sandplay. It is, without doubt, fascinating and intriguing to observe the process of sandplay and to conjecture what the miniatures might mean or what the scene might be saying. It is often possible to correctly interpret what is laid out in the sand. Whereas this helps us as counselors to know that progress is being made, interpretation is not necessarily appropriate in session with a couple. For example, Kalff (1980) cautioned appropriately against interpretation. It is also important to recognize that interpretation may often serve to meet the need of the counselor rather than the need of the client. In my experience, interpretation was truly helpful when the client or couple came up with the interpretation. By creating an environment for growth and healing to occur and taking the couple through the roadblocks and pain, the counselor may find that interpretation is not a decisive factor in the therapy.

I have found that it is helpful to take slides or pictures of the completed sand trays. Assuming that appropriate authorizations have been obtained, this provides a visual and chronological record of the therapy process, which I often share with my clients during and at the end of the therapy process as a means of progress review and discussion. Videotaping the sandplay sessions also is helpful for purposes of supervision and counselor development.

Conclusion

The challenges of couple conflicts are often easier to express, observe, and process through an expressive therapy such as sandplay. Like any other therapeutic approach or technique, however, sandplay does not provide all of the answers. Although the primary issues related to couple conflicts (e.g., money, sex, parenting) seem to remain stable, the challenges facing couples in crisis as well as counselors may be getting more complex. Verbalizing intrapsychic and interpersonal pain is never easy. Sandplay may be one tool that provides couples with a safe place—a level playing field, if you will—in which to "talk" about issues of great import. The interested reader is encouraged to seek the necessary training.

In my opinion, successful therapy with couples involves the counselor being a facilitator rather than a director of the process. The beauty of sandplay with couples is that this facilitation process is given wings. Sandplay maintains the focus on the process as opposed to the product.

References

Allan, J. (1988). *Inscapes of the child's world: Jungian counseling in schools and clinics*. Dallas, TX: Spring Publications.

Carey, L. (1990). Sandplay with a troubled child. *The Arts in Psychotherapy, 17,* 197–209.

Guerin, P., Fay, L., Burden, S., & Kautto, J. (1987). T*he evaluation and treatment of marital conflict.* New York: Basic Books.

Kalff, D. (1980). *Sandplay: A psychotherapeutic approach to the psyche.* Santa Monica, CA: Sigo Press.

Lowenfeld, M. (1979). *The world technique.* London: George Allen & Unwin.

Wells, H. G. (1911). *Floor games.* London: Palmer.

■ ■ ■

15

Create-a-Game

Karin B. Jordan, PhD

G ame playing, according to archeologists, can be traced back to 3,500 BC (Avedon & Sutton–Smith, 1971). The games we know today are believed to be rooted in the game of chess, which is a derivative of the Chinese war game Wei–Hai (Ellington, Addinall, & Percival, 1981; Smith-Ulione, 1983). Games are generally designed from a cultural perspective, providing an opportunity to practice skills and traits deemed desirable. For example, in the Inuit culture, cooperation is stressed as a way to win because it is an essential trait needed by this culture to survive the harsh Canadian Arctic climate (Melamed, 1980).

Game playing has been incorporated in child and adolescent therapy because counselors and therapists can determine through board games the child's level of intelligence, maturity, social skills, self-esteem, and emotional growth (Crocker & Wroblewski, 1975). Games also help counselors learn about the child's ability to cope and personality strengths and weaknesses (Frey, 1986). The therapeutic usefulness of board games is not limited to children and adolescents. It has been used effectively within the context of couple and family therapy. Board games, such as the Ungame© and the Talking, Feeling and Doing Game©, provide an opportunity for the players to come to terms with people in their environment and try out social roles and activities. Opie and Opie (1976) reported that "a game is one that frees the spirit. It allows for no cares but those fictitious ones generated by the game itself" (p. 394). Board games, in the context of therapy, are not only self-involving and cathartic but also fun and exciting (Fox, 1988; Proby & Furney, 1987; White & Davis, 1987). The aforementioned elements support the utility of using board games within the context of play therapy and couple and family therapy.

Four- and 5-year-old children begin playing board games in order to test their skills, not merely for amusement. Children at this age generally play to compete with their past achievements. The rules with this age group must be minimal, and they are often changed or violated. Card and guessing games are also appropriate. Older children (between 6 and 11 years) have an increased cognitive ability to think and reason (Piaget, 1962). Among other things, games for children at this age serve as tools for exercising impulse control and dealing with frustrations. Children in this age group generally follow rules rigidly. As children reach adolescence, they develop the capacity to strategize, think logically, and solve problems (Schaefer & Reid, 1986). Board games foster children's cognitive and social development, because they encourage children to think and problem-solve, and they involve the interaction of two or more people. I describe a technique in which counselors use commercial games or create their own board game to be used as a therapeutic medium.

To implement this game-playing strategy, the counselor can use the board of an already existing game or create a new one that can be coded by clients with artwork and stickers. Dice, plastic tokens, and game questions cards (3×5 cards) can be used as needed. The question cards are designed by the counselor to "tap in" to cognitive, affective, and behavioral aspects relevant to the client's treatment and counselor's understanding of the client's real-life situation. The cards are designed as open-ended statements ("The funniest thing I remember my Mom doing was . . ." "My biggest fear is . . .") that elicit client responses and generate discussions. Game rules (how to move around the board) are established through counselor and client negotiation (e.g., "Whenever you roll the dice and get a four, you must pick up a game card, read it, and answer the question"). When using this technique, it is important to remember that the number of players, difficulty of game questions, and rules established for the game can be modified to meet the developmental needs and individual issues of the players. This structural and highly interactive technique lends itself to assessing social interaction patterns; couple, family, and group dynamics; behavior feelings and distortions; and concerns that are difficult to discern or for which it is difficult to provide corrective feedback. The objective of this technique is client acquisition and application of social, interactive, cognitive, behavioral, and affective skills. The skills may be developed through Create-a-Game, both in the session and at home as an extension of the session.

Create-a-Game is a technique that can be used effectively with children (individually and in the group setting), couples, and families. To play this game, children must have gone beyond spontaneous, imaginative play and demonstrated organized rule-based play, and they must have adequate verbal and cognitive ability. When the game is played with children, rules need to be kept to a minimum and frequently modified. As children grow and develop, rules are followed more rigidly, and children expect others to do the same.

This technique can enhance traditional talk therapy often used in community agencies and private practice with adult clients. The combination game play and talk therapy can expedite and strengthen therapeutic change. It also can be used in play therapy with children, in school settings, community agencies, and private practice with adult clients because it provides an outlet for expression and release of emotions. In addition, it encourages therapeutic change by addressing issues that might be overlooked or otherwise met with resistance by clients. Using the game formula may temper resistance and allow for exploration of painful and difficult issues. Counselors should advise parents who want to play the game at home with their children that it might raise some painful or uncomfortable issues.

The primary advantage of using the Create-a-Game technique is its adaptability to the client's age, the presenting problem, and the therapeutic setting. This technique is nonthreatening, flexible, and fun. It is a useful means of engaging and releasing emotions, and it provides an opportunity to address issues within the context of a game that otherwise might not come up in traditional talk therapy. The technique is also cost effective for clinicians because, unlike expensive therapeutic games that often have limited range of use, Create-a-Game is inexpensive to create and may be adapted for use with a wide range of clients.

References

Avedon, B., & Sutton-Smith, B. (1971). *The study of games.* Toronto: Wiley.

Crocker, G. W., & Wroblewski, M. (1975). Using recreational games in counseling. *Personnel and Guidance Journal, 53,* 453–458.

Ellington, H., Addinall, B., & Percival, F. (1981). *Games and simulations in science education.* New York: Kogan Page.

Frey, D. E. (1986). Communication board games with children. In C. E. Schaefer & S. E. Reid (Eds.), *Game play: Therapeutic use of childhood games* (pp. 21–40). New York: Wiley.

Fox, H. (1988). Great games. *Learning, 17,* 66–67.

Melamed, L. (1980). Games for growth: A leading question. In P. Wilkinson (Ed.), *In celebration of play: An integrated approach to play and child development* (pp. 160–170). New York: St. Martin's Press.

Opie, I., & Opie, P. (1976). Street games: Counting out and chasing. In J. S. Brunner, A. Jolly, & K. Sylva (Eds.), *Play: Its role in development and evolution* (pp. 394–412). New York: Basic Books.

Piaget, J. (1962). *Play, dreams, and imitation in childhood.* New York: Norton.

Proby, M., & Furney, S. (1987). Nutrition review: A participation game. *Journal of School Health, 57,* 33–34.

Schaefer, C. E., & Reid, S. E. (Eds.). (1986). *Game play: Therapeutic use of childhood games.* New York: Wiley.

Smith-Ulione, M. (1983). Simulation in nursing education. *Journal of Nursing Education, 22,* 349–351.

White, G., & Davis, A. (1987). Teaching ethics using games. *Journal of Advanced Nursing, 12,* 621–624.

■ ■ ■

16

Permission to Speak Freely: Consent and Intervention With the Noncustodial Parent and Children

S. Allen Wilcoxon, EdD

Intervention with families experiencing divorce has been an area of emphasis within family therapy for many years. The primary focus of professional literature has been on work with the custodial parent and children as well as interventions with stepparents and stepchildren (Little, 1992; Nickerson, 1986). By contrast, writings concerning noncustodial parents have typically addressed more personal concerns such as losses, reduced contacts with their children, and similar issues (Brody & Forehand, 1990; Wallerstein & Kelly, 1980). Only occasional mention has been made of therapy for the unique configuration of the noncustodial parent and the children (Amato, 1986; Arditti, 1992; Seagull & Seagull, 1977). Specific examples of the issues they face include separation, loss, and grief within the early stages of divorce adjustment, needs of the children that are suited primarily for therapy with the noncustodial parent (e.g., death of a relative of the noncustodial parent, gender-role concerns, pending relocation of residence with the noncustodial parent), behavioral and communication difficulties in scheduled custody visits, anticipated changes with pronounced impact on both parent and child (e.g., relocation, remarriage, terminal illness;

Goldenberg & Goldenberg, 1998; Wilcoxon, 1994). Wilcoxon (1994) offered further comment on the unique legal, ethical, and practical considerations that one must examine in this somewhat unwieldy situation. The nature of such arrangements often evolves from the balance of legal consent from the custodial parent and interventions specifically geared for work with noncustodial parents and children. In this chapter I provide commentary and suggestions on issues of consent and intervention within this common yet atypical circumstance.

Considerations Regarding Parental Consent

For perspective, the practitioner pursuing consent for work with a noncustodial parent and his or her children would be well-advised to consider such requests as though the noncustodial parent was not a parent. In essence, parental status as tantamount to the capacity to provide consent cannot be assumed unless full joint custody exists. Otherwise, the request must be treated somewhat like a referral for which the practitioner must secure parental consent for further services. From the outset, the practitioner should clarify the nature of the custody agreement and its potential impact on therapy decisions by reviewing the divorce and custody settlement (Beis, 1984). A review of this document may verify claims of full joint custody or may indicate specific terms unique to the custody agreement. An understanding of the limitations of the divorce and custody agreement could greatly assist in treatment planning (e.g., "Since you can only be with your children on alternate weekends to attempt these changes, let's consider ways in which you can promote these changes both during these contacts and between visits").

The custodial parent should be involved in decisions regarding therapy for the children and the noncustodial parent. The stipulations of any custody agreement as well as the tradition of legal precedent typically favor the preferences of the custodial parent in consent issues affecting the minor children (Schweitzegebel & Schweitzegebel, 1980). Thus, it is necessary for the therapist to secure consent from the custodial parent prior to initiating services from which that parent is excluded. A battle for permission to pursue therapy may become a metaphor for extending divorce discord between former spouses. Were such an occasion to arise, permission to enter therapy might become an end in itself, thereby relegating actual intervention efforts to a secondary status. Practitioners should generally minimize their interaction with either parent during such a dispute, because the likelihood for subsequent contact with both adults is quite high. Parental consent for counseling may be unnecessary in some states, or legal officials may be enjoined by the noncustodial parent who is unable to secure consent from the former spouse. However, such pursuits should be viewed as last resorts rather than as initial tactics.

The most reasonable method for securing parental consent involves a two-step procedure. The initial step is for the therapist to provide a formal statement to the custodial parent about the request and the nature of services. Such information is typically reflected in a practice statement or disclosure document provided to clients at intake. However, additional information should be provided for the custodial parent's consideration and action. A summary of the nature of the request from the noncustodial parent (provided that the noncustodial parent has given permission) and a request for waiver of rights to compel disclosures (i.e., parental confidentiality) should also be provided to assure that confidentiality is maintained in the therapy relationship. Such agreements are common in therapy with children that excludes parents in settings such as schools and agencies. Although such a plan might prompt resentment from the noncustodial parent, it is an essential feature of the "battle for structure" (Napier & Whitaker, 1978, p. 10) between the clients and the therapist.

The second step in securing consent involves giving an opportunity for the custodial parent to engage in a dialogue with the practitioner about the request for services, preferably in the counselor's office. This opportunity is critical and innately delicate from a number of perspectives. The children should not participate at this juncture in order to avoid potentially troublesome confrontations or unnecessary conflicts. The noncustodial parent should also be excluded from this meeting in order to invite the cooperation of the custodial parent and to clarify the boundaries of the proposed therapy relationship. However, the rights belonging to the noncustodial parent (e.g., confidentiality) must not be sacrificed. A workable solution to this dilemma has been to audiotape the session with the understanding that the noncustodial parent may choose to review the tape. The focus of this session should be narrow and strict, with consent as the singular goal. The custodial parent should be assured that the focus of therapy is the relationship between the former spouse and the children and not the relationship between the former spouses. Similarly, the custodial parent should be assured that he or she will be contacted by the therapist in the event of a therapeutic concern that would require parental attention. Some custodial parents might be unwilling to agree to such limits. In such cases, an alternate solution might be to secure consent in exchange for regular reports from the practitioner regarding the progress of therapy, with special care taken not to jeopardize the confidentiality of sessions. Such an agreement would at least represent a good-faith effort to clarify limitations of confidentiality prior to initiating family therapy that would exclude this adult. However, this option should not be explored without thorough discussion between the practitioner and the noncustodial parent, preferably with legal counsel.

All agreements should be made in writing, with copies provided to both adults. Such "consent sessions" may involve as many as two occasions of dialogue with the professional and the custodial parent. Fees for "consent sessions" with the custodial parent should be paid by the noncustodial parent, because it is a crucial matter of management for the intervention requests. Moreover, no services to the children should be provided until all elements of consent are concluded.

Consent sessions should feature forethought about varied issues of intervention, including formal assurance of all fee obligations resting with the noncustodial parent and no contact with health care providers or similar agencies affiliated with the custodial household. Release of records on termination is of particular note in that recorded information pertinent to the care of minor children can be compelled for disclosure by the custodial parent. In this regard, separate case files for children and the noncustodial parent would be a safeguard to protect the privacy of information from sessions including only the parent.

Therapists and noncustodial parents should be aware that consent for services and waiver of confidentiality rights do not necessarily offset statutes in states that do not endorse privileged communication for the practitioner. Wilcoxon (1994) noted that in such instances, courtroom testimony and disclosures may be demanded of the practitioners who, despite protests to the contrary, are compelled to disclose information assumed to be confidential. Hence, this limitation of confidentiality should be discussed fully with the parent–client prior to initiating counseling services.

Intervention Issues and Considerations

The critical initial issue in requests for family therapy with noncustodial parents and their children is the basis for the request. Therapy related to issues of anger, sorrow, resentment, or similar concerns between former spouses generally is unproductive for family therapy involving the noncustodial parent and the children. In such cases, therapy becomes a formal and sanctioned medium through which unresolved adult issues are projected into the lives of the children, typically promoting confusion and resentment over parental loyalty. Similarly, discussions about dissatisfaction with custody agreements or visitation rights should be examined apart from children. By contrast, traditional concerns such as parenting, communication difficulties, pending changes, or general attempts to improve the adult–child relationship would be appropriate issues for intervention.

A significant and unique element of interventions with noncustodial parents and their children is stereotypical or biased thinking about their current familial circumstances (Kruk, 1991; Seagull & Seagull, 1977; Wall, 1992). Social notions of "the brave single parent," "the children from the broken home," "the former (noncustodial) parent," or "the lucky (noncustodial) parent who gets the kids for weekends without the hassles of real life" can permeate the attitudes of parents and children faced with divorce. Similarly, client attitudes that sustain these stereotypical expectations should be addressed, particularly in the early stages of divorce adjustment (e.g., "It sounds as though you believe 'Camp Daddy' is the only option for your weekends with your children" or "You sound as though you believe you can't burden your [noncustodial parent] with something like this because you have so little time with him or her"). Such stereotypes could hinder meaningful changes in the parent–child relationship.

Another element of intervention with this family system may be related to areas of lifestyles and disciplinary practices in the two residences. Whereas attempts to establish uniform rules and customs in the residences of both parents are often discussed, such consistency is relatively rare. The focus of interventions can easily move from discussions of preference (e.g., "This is the way I'd like it done") to discussions of comparison (e.g., "I don't really agree with what your [custodial parent] does and here's why"). Care should be taken to avoid the inevitable chaos arising from such comparisons; the focus should be on the rationale for preferences and attempts at compromise on lifestyles between the two residences.

If the noncustodial parent approaches the family practitioner with a request for therapy with his or her children and a similar therapy relationship is already in effect involving the custodial parent, children, and another practitioner, a decision to initiate a second relationship would be contraindicated. In such circumstances, participating in any efforts to convince the custodial parent that "fair is fair" would suggest that the primary issue is one of control rather than change for the noncustodial parent. Similarly, any therapy services that would include the custodial parent and their children should not be provided by the practitioner who has a prior relationship with the noncustodial parent and children (Adams, 1984).

Another practical issue for consideration is potential scheduling difficulties. When the custodial and noncustodial parents live in close proximity, regularly scheduled sessions during times other than those specified in custody and divorce agreements may be possible. These options should be examined with the custodial parent during "consent sessions." However, without legal sanction for such a schedule, the practitioner may encounter sporadic contact because the clients have no time. The practitioner serving such clients should expect to schedule sessions on Friday evenings or weekends. Therapy relationships may be discontinuous or relatively short-lived. In some instances, continuity may be maintained through a standing relationship with the noncustodial parent with intermittent sessions involving the children. Practitioners may find that brief therapy approaches and intersession homework (i.e., strategic approaches) rather than standard approaches are more likely to bring about change.

A similar practical concern for therapists serving the noncustodial parent and children is the potential for contact with the custodial parent. Wilcoxon (1994) noted that requests for disclosure, calls about comments from children following sessions with the noncustodial parent, attempts to "set the record straight" to clarify perceived misunderstandings on the part of the therapist, and similar reasons for communication from the custodial parent should be expected. In preparation for such instances, the practitioner should have ready access to the documents from consent sessions. Moreover, prior agreements to provide periodic, but limited, updates to the custodial parent may serve to offset unrequested assistance. The content of such discussions should be couched in reminders that prior agreements stipulated that confidentiality would be maintained except when the welfare of the children seems to be in jeopardy. The therapist must take great care not to triangulate the former spouse or to violate the boundary of the therapeutic relationship.

A related issue of considerable concern for serving this client population is the potential for withdrawal of consent to continue therapy services. The need to insure focused attention on the relationship issues between the noncustodial parent and children is substantively and practically reflected in this regard because withdrawal of consent would terminate services. The risk of losing consent for continuing services should not intimidate practitioner or parent, but the reality of this special circumstance should serve to focus the therapy agenda to exclude items that might affect the relationship in the custodial residence. In fact, improvements in the noncustodial parent's relationship with the children might even threaten the relationship between the children and custodial parent (Dominic & Schlesinger, 1980; Jacobs, 1982), possibly leading to threatened withdrawal of consent. Regardless of the case, subsequent "consent sessions" may even be in order to maintain the option for working with the noncustodial parent and children and, possibly, to provide a referral for services should the custodial parent present concerns warranting intervention. If this happens, however, the current practitioner should be prepared for interrupting or terminating services with the noncustodial family system to avoid duplication of services.

Conclusion

Other practical considerations for serving noncustodial parents and their children include referrals, decisions involving inclusion or exclusion of other family members or intimate partners of the noncustodial parent in therapy, and follow-up contacts with the custodial parent. Clearly, the unconventional nature of serving the noncustodial family system creates unique circumstances and considerations for professional intervention. For therapists working with this group of clients, consultation with both colleagues and legal counsel would seem to be a reasonable precaution. However, difficulties notwithstanding, the unique and unaddressed nature of this common circumstance compels attention and care from the practitioner community. When one secures "permission to speak freely," intervention efforts may be meaningful and significant.

References

Adams, P. L. (1984). Fathers absent and present. *Canadian Journal of Psychiatry, 29,* 228–223.

Amato, P. R. (1986). Father involvement and the self-esteem of children and adolescents. *Australian Journal of Sex, Marriage and Family, 7,* 6–16.

Arditti, J. A. (1992). Differences between fathers with joint custody and noncustodial fathers. *American Journal of Orthopsychiatry, 62,* 186–195.

Beis, E. B. (1984). *Mental health law*. Rockville, MD: Aspen.

Brody, G., & Forehand, R. (1990). Interparental conflict, relationship with the noncustodial father, and adolescent post-divorce adjustment. *Journal of Applied Developmental Psychology, 11*, 139–147.

Dominic, K. T., & Schlesinger, B. (1980). Weekend fathers: Family shadows. *Journal of Divorce, 3*, 241–247.

Goldenberg, H., & Goldenberg, I. (1998). *Counseling today's families* (3rd ed.). Pacific Grove, CA: Brooks/Cole.

Jacobs, J. W. (1982). The effect of divorce on fathers: An overview of the literature. *American Journal of Psychiatry, 139*, 1235–1241.

Kruk, E. (1991). Discontinuity between pre- and post-divorce father–child relationships: New evidence regarding paternal disengagement. *Journal of Divorce and Remarriage, 16*(3–4), 195–227.

Little, M. A. (1992). The impact of the custody plan on the family: A five-year follow-up (Executive summary). *Family and Conciliation Courts Review, 30*, 243–251.

Napier, A., & Whitaker, C. (1978). *The family crucible*. New York: Harper & Row.

Nickerson, E. T. (1986). Integrating the child into family therapy: The remaking of a for-adults-only orientation. *International Journal of Family Psychiatry, 7*, 59–69.

Schweitzegebel, R. L., & Schweitzebel, R. K. (1980). *Law and psychological practice*. New York: Wiley.

Seagull, A. A., & Seagull, E. A. (1977). The non-custodial father's relationship to his child: Conflicts and solutions. *Journal of Clinical Child Psychology, 6*, 11–15.

Wall, J. C. (1992). Maintaining the connection: Parenting as a noncustodial father. *Child and Adolescent Social Work Journal, 9*, 441–456.

Wallerstein, J. S., & Kelly, J. B. (1980). Effects of divorce on the visiting father–child relationship. *American Journal of Psychiatry, 137*, 1534–1539.

Wilcoxon, S. A. (1994). Family therapy with the noncustodial parent and children: Unique preliminary considerations. *Family Therapy, 21*, 107–115.

■ ■ ■

17

The School-Based Family Counseling Classroom Checklist Procedure

Michael J. Carter, PhD
and William P. Evans, PhD

Families play a pivotal role in the academic success of children (Dwyer & Hecht, 1992; Teachman, Day, & Carver, 1995; Turnbull & Turnbull, 1990). Many families, however, may not understand the degree to which family factors influence academic success or the importance of family involvement in children's education (Delgado-Gaitan & Allexsaht-Snider, 1992; Lord, Eccles, & McCarthy, 1994). In addition, many obstacles inhibit the ability of families and schools to develop strong partnerships, including cultural and language barriers, ineffective communication between home and school, and the inability of many parents to attend school meetings because of work and child care responsibilities (Chaskin & Richman, 1992; Friesen & Osher, 1996). To facilitate parental involvement, some schools have implemented the concept of school-based family counseling (SBFC), in which counselors work directly with families at the school site (Carter & Evans, 1995; Evans & Carter, 1997). The primary focus of SBFC is to create a family–school partnership that removes barriers to student achievement through a systemic problem-solving process.

A SBFC model for addressing classroom difficulties is described in detail elsewhere (Carter & Evans, 1995; Evans & Carter, 1997). This model actively involves the student, parent, and teacher in a shared problem-solving process that incorporates the various viewpoints of classroom problems into workable solutions. In general, emphasis is placed on developing specific strategies to improve classroom behavior while simultaneously addressing individual, family or school dynamics that may contribute to the problem. This classroom-focused family intervention process combines an ecological-systems perspective with a cognitive–behavioral paradigm for effecting behavior change in children (Christenson & Conoley, 1992; Fine & Carlson, 1992; Santostefano, 1985).

A specific technique that we have found useful in the context of elementary school counseling is the SBFC classroom checklist procedure (see Figure 17.1). This procedure uses a checklist as a vehicle for addressing barriers to learning by increasing student and parental awareness of classroom behavior. In addition, the checklist is used to improve the parent–child relationship through activation of a team approach to constructively address problems. The checklist also provides feedback to monitor the effectiveness of the classroom-focused intervention strategies. This procedure can also provide structured opportunities for parents and children to spend time together acknowledging progress, addressing developmental challenges, and nurturing their relationship.

Specifically, the procedure involves (a) transforming a negative operational definition of the classroom problem into a positive behavior that can be clearly demonstrated (e.g., "getting out of seat and disrupting class" into "stays in seat"); (b) identifying cognitive strategies that the student can use to produce the positive behavior (e.g., "If I stay in my seat, I'll beat the heat"); (c) assisting parents to help the student consistently implement the strategies in the classroom (e.g., nightly meetings between parents and child to review checklist and rehearse strategies); and (d) monitoring progress, identifying obstacles to success, and facilitating a problem-solving approach to address these. This intervention provides parents with a specific means of addressing child problems in a constructive manner that emphasizes the positive aspects of the child and the benefits of family involvement in overcoming obstacles to academic and social learning.

The checklist is designed to help the child, parents, and teacher to assess the child's behavior in the classroom, with particular emphasis on those behaviors that are most disruptive to the child and those around him or her. It is primarily used for the

FIGURE 17.1
The School-Based Family Counseling Classroom Checklist

The SBFC Classroom Checklist				
Name:_____ Date:_____	**TARGET BEHAVIORS**			
CLASSROOM SUBJECTS				TEACHER/ COMMENTS
TOTAL				

self-contained, elementary school classroom where all academic subjects are taught in the same classroom. An important aspect of this checklist is that it minimizes the time and energy spent by the teacher in providing feedback to the student and parent. The teacher is asked to evaluate three targeted behaviors at the end of each subject period but does not have to mark this checklist unless he or she has noticed a problem during that time. The parents and child are exclusively responsible for providing, collecting, and bringing home the checklist for parent–child review. This requires the parents and child to address core family issues such as assignment of tasks, compliance, and consistent follow-through. Difficulties in meeting this requirement may provide additional motivation for the family to work with the counselor on underlying family dynamics.

Procedure

The checklist is divided into a grid with date, child's name, and the teacher's name at the top. Along the left-hand side of the grid are the subjects that are taught daily in chronological order from top to bottom, with a TOTAL heading at the bottom left. The school day is divided into these subject headings versus time periods because elementary school teachers seem to be more cognizant of transitions between subject areas than the time on the clock. Across the top of the grid (left to right) are the three major behaviors of focus stated in positive operational terms. For example, "calling out answers" would be stated "raises hand and waits to be called on before speaking." At the far right-hand side of the page would be room for "any additional comments from teacher." It is important that the number of target behaviors be limited to a maximum of three so that implementation of the checklist is manageable for the teacher and family. This may require the parent–teacher–child team to prioritize the presenting problems.

The checklist is used to provide a clear picture of the child's current classroom behavior. We have used the checklist in the following manner:

1. Upon entering the classroom in the morning, the child is required by the parents to give the checklist to the teacher before instruction begins. The checklist must be easily accessible to the teacher, but confidentiality should be safeguarded (e.g., in the teacher's desk).
2. At the conclusion of each subject period, the teacher stops for a moment and evaluates whether the student has had any problem demonstrating the three target behaviors. If the child has had any difficulty, the teacher makes a mark in the box space corresponding to the target behavior for that subject. If no problem is evident, then the teacher resumes instruction without making any notation. If the teacher wishes to provide any comments concerning the child's behavior, space is provided at the far right-hand side of the checklist on the same line as the box; writing comments is entirely optional.
3. At the end of the school day, the child is required by the parents to secure the checklist from the teacher and bring it home for review. That afternoon or evening, a specific time is scheduled for a parent and the child to review the checklist.
4. The parents begin the review by having the child fill in all empty boxes with stars, happy faces, or other symbols of

success. The parents should acknowledge this success in a genuine and heartfelt manner that is meaningful to the child. This may be difficult for some parents, and the counselor may need to provide specific training so that they can effectively communicate their positive feelings about the child's success, no matter how limited it may appear. The acknowledgment of any successful classroom behavior is critical to effecting meaningful long-term change and cannot be overemphasized to parents. This is the cornerstone of the checklist technique. After filling in all of the empty boxes, the number of stars are added up for each target behavior and written at the bottom of the column.

5. After acknowledging successful target behaviors in the classroom, the parents then assist the child to explore the times during the day that the child was not able to achieve the target behaviors (where the teacher has marked the box). The child is asked to try to remember when these instances occurred (association with the subject area may be helpful) and to think about what might have happened to prevent him or her from demonstrating the target behavior. If specific cognitive strategies to increase the target behaviors have been developed, then the parent can coach the child in how to use these the next day during that subject. The checklist is then kept in a notebook for subsequent evaluation of long-term progress with the teacher and counselor.

During this discussion, the parents must take great care to avoid criticizing the child, trying to find blame, or other negative reactions. This is critical because the goal of this review is to help the child assess experiences of success and challenges in a nonemotional manner conducive to learning. If the child experiences negative emotions from the parents, his or her availability for learning during this review may be reduced and any negative self-image may be reinforced. The parents must proactively model for the child a positive and optimistic approach to solving problems. No matter what the ratio of success to failure, the parents are responsible for making the child feel that this time spent together was constructive and nurturing, not critical or punitive. The counselor is responsible for assessing the extent to which the parents experience any difficulties in this regard and addressing it when necessary. In many ways these issues constitute the core elements of counseling families with school-aged children, and the checklist procedure may help the counselor to increase the family's awareness of these dynamics.

Conclusion

Numerous behavior rating scales have been developed as a quick and valid means of gaining information regarding children's social and academic behavior (Ben-Porath, Williams, & Uchiyama, 1989; Carlson & Lahey, 1983; Elliot, Buss, & Gresham, 1993; Gresham, 1985). This information often is used to develop treatment and intervention strategies. The SBFC checklist procedure, however, combines an ongoing assessment function with the counseling process to improve the parent–child relationship and increase parental participation in academic and social development. The successful implementation of this technique requires the family to work together as a unit, which is typically a primary goal of family systems interventions. The counselor must be effective in assisting the family to confront and resolve a variety of systemic problems, some of which may not be known to them. This checklist procedure may provide concrete and meaningful information for the family and can be used to explore family factors that may affect educational success. These include the ability of the parental subsystem to set limits and provide consistent positive and negative consequences for children, the level of involvement that siblings and other family members have in modeling and encouraging appropriate behavior, and the development of strategies to reduce conflict in the home in order to enhance learning. Although this procedure does require teacher energy and time, teachers report that this brief, periodic assessment is easy to complete and results in significant improvements in student behavior and parental support. This procedure could also be useful for counselors not practicing at the school site, but it does require at least one consultation meeting with the teacher, parent, and child to develop the target behaviors and set up the process.

References

Ben-Porath, Y. S., Williams, C. L., & Uchiyama, C. (1989). New scales for the Devereux Adolescent Behavior Rating Scale. *Psychological Assessment, 1*, 58–60.

Carlson, C. L., & Lahey, B. B. (1983). Factor structure of teacher rating scales. *School Psychology Review, 12*, 285–292.

Carter, M. J., & Evans, W. P. (1995). School-based family counseling: Helping teachers improve student success in the urban classroom. *National Forum of Teacher Education Journal, 5*, 3–11.

Chaskin, R. J., & Richman, H. A. (1992). Concerns about school-linked services: Institution versus community-based models. *The Future of Children, 2,* 107–117.

Christenson, S. L., & Conoley, J. C. (Eds.). (1992). *Home–school collaboration: Enhancing children's academic and social competence.* Silver Spring, MD: NASP Publications.

Delgado-Gaitan, C., & Allexsaht-Snider, M. (1992). Mediating school cultural knowledge for children: The parent's role. In H. J. Johnston (Ed.), *Effective schooling strategies for economically dependent students: School-based strategies for diverse student populations* (pp.79–95). Norwood, NJ: Ablex.

Dwyer, D. J., & Hecht, J. B. (1992). Minimal parental involvement. *The School Community Journal, 2,* 53–66.

Elliot, S., Buss, R. T., & Gresham, F. M. (1993). Behavior rating scales: Issues of use and development. *School Psychology Review, 22,* 313–321.

Evans, W. P., & Carter, M. J. (1997). Urban school-based family counseling: Role definition, practice applications, and training implications. *Journal of Counseling and Development, 75,* 366–374.

Fine, M. J., & Carlson, C. (Eds.). (1992). *The handbook of family–school intervention: A systems perspective.* Boston: Allyn & Bacon.

Friesen, B. J., & Osher, T. W. (1996). Involving families in change: Challenges and opportunities. *Special Services in the Schools, 11,* 187–201.

Gresham, F. M. (1985). Conceptual issues in the assessment of social competence in children. In P. S. Strain, M. J. Guralnick, & H. M. Walker (Eds.), *Children's social behavior: Development, assessment, and modification* (pp. 143–213). New York: Academic Press.

Lord, S. E., Eccles, J. S., & McCarthy, K. A. (1994). Surviving the junior high school transition: Family processes and self-perceptions as protective and risk factors. *Journal of Early Adolescence, 14,* 166–199.

Santostefano, S. (1985). *Cognitive control therapy with children and adolescents.* Elmsford, NY: Pergamon Press.

Teachman, J. D., Day, R. D., & Carver, K. P. (1995). The impact of family environment on educational attainment: Do families make a difference? In B. A. Ryan, G. R. Adams, T. P. Gullotta, R. P. Weissberg, & R. L. Hampton (Eds.), *The family–school connection* (pp. 155–203). Thousand Oaks, CA: Sage.

Turnbull, A. P., & Turnbull, H. R. (1990). *Families, professionals, and exceptionality: A special partnership.* Columbus, OH: Merrill.

■ ■ ■

18

Emotional Balancing: A Parenting Technique to Enhance Parent–Child Relationships

Michael S. Nystul, PhD

Educating parents and altering parent–child interactions is an effective way to help children overcome problematic behavior (Mooney, 1995). According to Mooney, the two most common forms of parent education involve changing behavior and fostering democratic family living; such approaches are described in *Parent Effectiveness Training* (Gordon, 1970) and *Systematic Training for Effective Parenting: The Parent's Handbook* (Dinkmeyer & McKay, 1989).

Behavioral and "democratic"-oriented parent education programs tend to focus on helping parents develop appropriate behaviors and attitudes. For example, behavioral programs help parents implement behavior modification principles, and the systematic training for effective parenting (STEP) program promotes positive parental attitudes such as showing respect and having the courage to admit imperfections.

Parental emotion seems to be a dimension to parenting that has received relatively little attention in the literature. The purpose of this chapter is to address this neglected area of parenting by describing the use of the parenting technique *emotional balancing.*

Emotional balancing is a parenting technique that fosters family cohesion and affective involvement enabling children and adolescents to develop as responsible and autonomous individuals. The theoretical origins of emotional balancing can be traced to the pioneering work of Salvador Minuchin (1974). Minuchin's concept of boundaries provides a basic framework for conceptualizing emotional balancing. Boundaries are the unwritten rules that determine who and how family members participate in family life. Minuchin described boundaries in terms of a continuum from disengaged to enmeshed, with clear boundaries occupying the middle of the continuum. Disengaged boundaries are "rigid," that is, they do not adjust to the emerging needs of the family system, resulting in detached or disengaged family members. Enmeshed boundaries are essentially the opposite of disengaged boundaries. They are "diffused," lacking a clear sense of the role and function that family members have in relation to one another. Clear boundaries represent the middle ground or healthy range between these two extremes; they reflect mutually understood expectations that family members have of one another and facilitate unobstructed participation in family life.

Barber and Buehler (1996) identified several other theories that have expanded on Minuchin's (1974) theory. Olson, Russell, and Sprenkle (1983) proposed a model based on the concept of family cohesion, with *cohesion* defined as the degree of emotional bonding between family members. Low levels of cohesion represent disengagement, and high levels indicate enmeshment. Both extremes are considered dysfunctional; they contribute either to isolation (disengagement) or overinvolvement (enmeshment) between family members. Moderate levels of cohesion are considered ideal—they allow for emotional bonding and support while also permitting individualization and differentiation between family members.

Epstein, Bishop, and Baldwin (1982) developed another post-Minuchin (1974) theory. Their theory was based on the concept of *affective involvement,* the degree of emotional engagement between family members. According to this theory, there are six levels of affective involvement: lack of involvement, involvement with no feeling, narcissistic involvement, empathic involvement, overinvolvement, and symbiotic involvement. Empathic involvement is considered ideal and involves communicating love, caring, and compassion to family members.

Parental Emotions Model

The theories of Minuchin (1974), Olson et al. (1983), and Epstein et al. (1982) can be integrated to describe the role of parental emotions in parenting. The parental emotions model suggests that parents should avoid engaging in the extremes of emotional disengagement and emotional enmeshment. Emotional disengagement occurs when parents withdraw emotionally from their child or adolescent. They may be discouraged and are basically saying, "I've had enough. . . . I just don't care anymore." This can be considered a form of emotional abandonment. Parents may resort to this negative affect as a means of coping with the frustration, hurt, and disappointment associated with parenting.

Emotional enmeshment represents the other emotional extreme in parenting. It occurs when parents become overly emotionally involved to the extent that their emotions are interfering with their children's ability to become responsible and autonomous persons.

Emotional balance is the range of parental emotions that lies between emotional disengagement and emotional enmeshment. Emotional balance is characterized by a moderate level of cohesion or relatedness between family members. Emotionally balanced parents are involved in the activities and interests of their children in a manner that is not overly intrusive or overly detached. Emotional balance represents a well-functioning level of affective involvement communicating positive and negative emotions such as love, support, caring, anger, and disappointment while still allowing for individualization of family members.

Emotional balance can be maintained by communicating emotions on different levels of intensity depending on the situation. Low to moderate levels of intensity can be useful to create "emotional space" for a family member to develop autonomy and individual responsibility. High levels of emotional intensity can be necessary to get a family member's attention and to communicate clearly a parent's concern (e.g., when an adolescent takes a car without permission and stays out late).

The key to maintaining emotional balance (in terms of emotional intensity) is not only what you communicate but also how you communicate. The appropriate "how" of communicating emotional intensity can be fostered by facilitative processes such as maintaining "core conditions" in the parent–child relationship and using effective communication skills. Examples of these core conditions include unconditional love (always communicating love and understanding and also being able to "separate the deed from the doer"); communicating respect, caring, compassion, and empathy; and promoting responsible and autonomous development (by focusing on choices and responsibility). These conditions help children and adolescents to know that their parents care about them and want what is best for them, and this promotes a positive parent–child bond.

Emotional intensity is appropriately communicated through the use of effective communication skills such as being clear, specific, constructive, and relational. An example of this type of communication is in the use of "I" messages instead of "you" messages (see Dinkmeyer & McKay, 1989). "I" messages are relational, because they communicate how the parent feels in relation to the child or adolescent. They are also clear, specific, and constructive, because they tell the child clearly and specifically what behavior is problematic, and why the parent finds the behavior troubling. For example, the parent could use an "I" message to communicate high levels of emotional intensity with the adolescent who took the car and stayed out late by saying, "I really get angry when you do things you know you are not supposed to do. I feel its disrespectful to me, creates needless worry for me, and could result in something terrible happening to you, like getting into a wreck." "I" messages should be constructed to foster constructive outcomes, whereby children can learn from their choices and become responsible and autonomous individuals. "I" messages should also be designed to help children become aware of how their behavior affects others in terms of the anger or other emotions the parent may be experiencing. "You" messages are not relational and tend to be destructive attacks on the child. A "you" message in this example could be, "You really are an inconsiderate little jerk. You have really done it this time, taking the car without asking. Now, you are going to get grounded for a month."

Inappropriate communication of emotional intensity is communication that does not include facilitative processes such as the "core conditions" in the parent–child relationships or effective communication skills such as the use of "I" messages. Without positive communication processes, parents can easily let low levels of emotional intensity become emotional disengagement, and high levels of emotional intensity can become emotional enmeshment. For example, parents who do not communicate caring or compassion to their children may psychologically distance themselves to the point where they may lose interest and become disengaged. At the other extreme, parents who are inappropriate with their emotional intensity (e.g., use "you" messages to attack or pity their children) may end up in an emotionally enmeshed position and rob their children of a chance to become aware of choices and assume responsibility for their behavior.

Emotional Balancing Procedure

The parenting technique of emotional balancing is composed of several steps or procedures that are adjusted and modified as necessary to meet the unique needs of children and adolescents. The steps associated with helping parents create an emotional balance are as follows.

1. Provide an overview of the role of parental emotions in parenting and assess where the parents function emotionally, including information on emotional disengagement, emotional enmeshment, and emotional balancing. Handouts and other reading material can be useful in this process. Moreover, provide an opportunity for parents to determine where they tend to function emotionally with their children.
2. Explore systemic issues as needed. Family systems theory suggests that any change within the family system has an effect on the family system as a whole. Parents should be encouraged to develop a systemic perspective for assessing emotional responses. For example, when one parent goes to one emotional extreme (such as emotional enmeshment), it is not uncommon for the other parent to go to the other emotional extreme (i.e., emotional disengagement). This could occur when the enmeshed parent (out of sympathy or guilt from an experience such as a divorce) continues to give in to a child who has misbehaved. The other parent could get discouraged and become emotionally disengaged, thinking: "If my spouse keeps giving in, why I should even bother to try and discipline the child?" A parent may be even more prone to disengage if he or she is a stepparent and conclude, "It's not my child, so it's none of my business anyway. And I don't want to interfere."
3. Provide appropriate parenting intervention as necessary. Appropriate intervention procedures can then be identified to help parents move toward emotional balance. For example, counseling or parent education could be directed at helping parents overcome feelings of discouragement, so they can move from emotional disengagement to emotional balance.

Applications of Emotional Balancing

Emotional balancing may be useful for all aspects of parenting, particularly in matters of discipline. Children and adolescents (and all people, for that matter) may not accept responsibility for their mistakes and opt to externalize and blame others for their failures. The challenge for parents is to help their children or adolescents become aware of the choices they made and accept responsibility for them.

Emotionally enmeshed or disengaged parents may have difficulty helping their children become responsible. A disengaged parent may not be aware of what is going on and therefore may not take appropriate corrective measures. The enmeshed parent may become emotionally overinvolved, resulting in different potential discipline problems depending on the emotion. For example, excessive anger and extreme punitiveness can be especially problematic (e.g., arguing with a child and grounding the child for a month). When a parent does this, the child may argue with the parent and say how unfair the parent is regarding the length of the grounding, thereby losing an opportunity to have the child focus on the misbehavior; instead, the focus shifts to parental unfairness or some related topic.

Children and adolescents welcome these arguments as convenient diversions from having to take responsibility for the poor choices they have made. Taking responsibility is usually the last thing they want to do; they typically prefer to blame others for their unhappiness. When this happens, the parent becomes an easy scapegoat for the child or adolescent.

Conclusion

Parents may function at one extreme or fluctuate between the two extremes of parental emotions (i.e., emotional disengagement and emotional enmeshment). When this occurs, they require help to get emotionally balanced. The emotional balancing procedure described in this chapter can help parents make an appropriate emotional connection with their children. It involves getting appropriately involved with the child's or adolescent's interests. In addition, parents can communicate a full range of emotions such as love, caring, anger, and disappointment at varying levels of intensity (ranging from low to high). Emotional balancing can involve creating "emotional space" so children and adolescents can learn to assume responsibility for their choices and become autonomous and responsible individuals.

References

Barber, B. K., & Buehler, C. (1996). Family cohesion and enmeshment: Different constructs, different effect. *Journal of Marriage and the Family, 58*, 433–441.

Dinkmeyer, D., & McKay, G. D. (1989). *Systematic training for effective parenting: The parent's handbook.* Circle Pines, MN: American Guidance Service.

Epstein, N. B., Bishop, D. S., & Baldwin, L. M. (1982). McMaster model of family functioning: A view of the normal family. In F. Walsh (Ed.), *Normal family processes* (pp. 115–141). New York: Guilford Press.

Gordon, T. (1970). *Parent effectiveness training.* New York: Wyden.

Minuchin, S. (1974). *Families and family therapy.* Cambridge, MA: Harvard University Press.

Mooney, S. (1995). Parent training: A review of Adlerian, parent effectiveness, and behavioral research. *The Family Journal: Counseling and Therapy for Couples and Families, 3*, 218–230.

Olson, D. H., Russell, C. S., & Sprenkle, D. H. (1983). Circumplex model of parental and family systems: VI. Theoretical update. *Family Process, 22*, 69–83.

■ ■ ■

19

How Was Your Day? Using Questions About the Family's Daily Routine

Frances Y. Mullis, PhD

The technique of asking questions about the daily routine in the home is often used by counselors to assess the relationship between parents and children and between the siblings (Rosenberg, 1971; Sweeney, 1998; Walton, 1980). Counselors who work from an Adlerian perspective frequently use daily routine questions to ascertain either the lifestyle (the Adlerian nomenclature for personality; Sweeney, 1998) or the mistaken goal of behavior (attention, power, revenge, avoiding failure) of the child about whom the parents are most concerned. Regardless of the counselor's theoretical orientation, this type of questioning can provide useful information not only about children's mistaken goals, but also about parental roles, expectations, problem-solving strategies, family activities, and feelings of encouragement or discouragement in the family as a whole. In addition, these questions often provide an opportunity for the counselor to empathize with the family and to find ways to deliberately encourage family members.

Useful Questions

The kinds of questions that can be used to elicit information about the family's daily routine are presented below.

1. How does the child get up in the morning?
   - Who awakens the child? Is he or she called more than once? How many times?
   - What about dressing? Who selects the clothes to be worn? Does the child dress himself or herself?
   - What about the use of the bathroom? Does the child need help washing? Brushing teeth?
   - What about breakfast? Who fixes breakfast? Does the child eat a "good" breakfast?

2. How does the child get off to school?
   - Does he or she ride the bus?
   - Who makes certain homework, books, and lunch money are ready?
   - What happens if the child forgets something?

3. How does dinner go?
   - Does the child have responsibilities, such as setting the table, clearing the table, doing dishes?
   - Does he or she eat a "good" dinner?

4. How is homework handled?
   - Is a specific time and place set for doing homework?
   - Does the child have to be reminded to do homework?
   - Does the child need help with homework?

5. How does bedtime go?
   - What time is bedtime?
   - Is there a bedtime ritual?

As questions are asked about the daily routine, the counselor follows up with questions such as "How did you handle that?", "How did that work?", "What else have you tried?", and "Whose idea was that?" In addition, many opportunities are provided for the counselor to empathize with the family and their concerns.

Mistaken Goals of Behavior

If the questions are being used to help determine the child's mistaken goal of behavior, it is important for the counselor to ask the parents how they feel when that behavior occurs, what they do about the behavior, and how the child responds to them. According to Adlerian theory (Sweeney, 1998), children who seek undue attention typically bring about feelings of irritation or annoyance in adults and stop the behavior for a short time after being reprimanded. When children derive a feeling of power from the behavior, adults usually feel angry or challenged. The behavior tends to intensify when the child is reprimanded. Children who seek revenge often attempt to hurt others because they believe they have been hurt. Adults who interact with revenge-seeking children often feel hurt and may even dislike the children. Children who seek revenge intensify the misbehavior when corrected, as do power-seeking children. Children whose goal is to avoid failure do nothing to elicit reprimands, and attempts by parents to change their children's behavior are usually unsuccessful and result in parental feelings of helplessness and concern.

If questions about getting children up in the morning elicit answers that indicate that the parent struggles to get the child out of bed, for example, and feels angry about the struggle, the child may be seeking power. Asking how the parent handles other problem behaviors may help to verify this hypothesis about the parent–child interaction. Throughout the series of questions, the counselor should be alert for patterns and sequences of interaction between the parent and child, between siblings, and between parents or other adults in the household.

Parental Roles

All families must fulfill various family functions, such as providing nurturing and support and providing resources (food, clothing, and shelter). The repetitive behavior patterns whereby family members carry out these functions are called family roles (Epstein, Bishop, Ryan, Miller, & Keitner, 1993). Although roles are useful for efficient and effective family functioning, it is important for the counselor to explore how roles are assigned and how satisfied family members are with the roles assigned to them. A common pattern that may lead to dissatisfaction is assigning tasks according to stereotypical gender roles. Friction between the parents can arise if both parents work outside the home, but the mother is always the one who is assigned the task of making certain that everyone gets up, eats breakfast, and leaves the house on time with homework and lunches. A discussion of task reassignment could be useful, with the father becoming more involved in the morning routine, or with both parents relinquishing responsibility to the children in the family. In single-parent families, it is also critical to help the parent determine how roles may be assigned so that the daily routine is less stressful for the adult.

Expectations

Discovering who is responsible for daily tasks can provide the counselor with important information about parental expectations. If parents are expecting too much of a young child, or not enough of an older child, providing information about child development may be in order. A pampering relationship between the parent and child, in which the parent takes over tasks the child could easily perform, is a common occurrence in many households. This type of parental behavior can lead to feelings of entitlement or to lowered self-esteem in the child.

If parental expectations seem to be an area needing further exploration, it can be helpful to determine the source of the expectations. Expectations often are based on those of one's grandparents or society in general. For example, parents may expect boys to be athletic, and they may have difficulty accepting a son who does not enjoy sports. Unfulfilled wishes from the parents' past may also influence expectations. Parents who dreamed of being able to play a musical instrument but could not afford lessons when they were children may be angry with their own child who does not want to take music lessons even though the parents can afford to provide them.

Problem-Solving Strategies

The answers to questions about the daily routine can yield a wealth of information about problem-solving strategies used by the parents. When a problem area surfaces, the counselor can ask questions such as "When he or she does that, how do you feel?", "How do you handle that?", and "What does the child do then?" Other questions can be asked to determine whether the parents' answer is the usual method of handling problems and whether that strategy works. If the strategy is not effective, parents can be asked if they have thought of other techniques that they might try. In this way, the counselor can determine the range of responses available to the parents and may decide that information about discipline techniques is warranted.

Family Activities

By assessing the family's daily routine, the counselor can also discover how much time the family has for fun; especially for enjoyable activities in which everyone participates. In some families, particularly those with single parents, little time is available for having fun together. When describing the daily routine, it may sound as if the day is hectic from beginning to end. If it sounds hectic to the counselor or therapist, then it probably seems that way to the family. An important counseling intervention could be to help the family decide how to find time to add pleasurable activities to their schedule. If the parents are taking on responsibilities that belong to the children, they might offer as an incentive for the children to become more responsible the anticipation of family fun time.

Suggesting simple rituals, such as a bedtime ritual, could also add a few minutes of relaxation time for the family. Bedtime rituals contribute to feelings of security and comfort for children (Mullis & Fincher, 1996), and the more families use rituals, such as customary mealtimes, bedtime routines, and everyday greetings and farewells, the higher their ratings of overall family adjustment (Sprunger, Boyce, & Gaines, 1985).

Discouragement and Encouragement

As the counselor asks questions about the daily routine, he or she can be mindful of areas of discouragement and of aspects of family life that are encouraging to both parents and children. Consequently, opportunities arise for the counselor to purposefully encourage the family. For example, if a family has worked out a solution to a problem with chores, a comment can be made such as "It sounds as if you've been able to talk together and share ideas so that you found a solution you can all live with. That's a helpful thing to be able to do." Not only has the family been encouraged about their handling of this specific dilemma, but the suggestion has also been made that this technique can be used to solve other problems.

Families in counseling are usually discouraged. Finding aspects of family life that are going well and pointing out those particular strengths can be very helpful for families who are struggling to change.

Conclusion

Questions about the family's daily routine can be very revealing for both the family and the family counselor. Talking through the daily routine can be eye opening to the parents because it may illuminate their patterns of interaction with their children or indicate how stressful their typical day is. For the counselor, this simple and nonthreatening set of questions provides a wealth of information, not only by furnishing specific data about the family, but also by directing attention to other areas that require exploration.

References

Epstein, N., Bishop, D., Ryan, C., Miller, I., & Keitner, G. (1993). The McMaster model view of healthy family functioning. In F. Walsh (Ed.), *Normal family processes* (2nd ed., pp. 138–160). New York: Guilford Press.

Mullis, F., & Fincher, S. F. (1996). Using rituals to define the school community. *Elementary School Guidance & Counseling, 30,* 243–251.

Rosenberg, B. (1971). Family counseling. In A. G. Nikelly (Ed.), *Techniques for behavior change* (pp. 117–123). Springfield, IL: Charles C Thomas.

Sprunger, L. W., Boyce, W. T., & Gaines, J. A. (1985). Family–infant congruence: Routines and rhythmicity in family adaptations to a young infant. *Child Development, 56,* 564–572.

Sweeney, T. J. (1998). *Adlerian counseling: A practitioner's approach* (4th ed.). Philadelphia: Accelerated Development and Taylor & Francis.

Walton, F. X. (1980). *Winning teenagers over in home and school: A manual for parents, teachers, counselors, and principals.* Columbia, SC: Adlerian Childcare Books.

■ ■ ■